THE JESUITS IN POLAND

THE

JESUITS IN POLAND

THE LOTHIAN ESSAY, 1892

BY

A. F. POLLARD, B.A.

JESUS COLLEGE, OXFORD

HASKELL HOUSE PUBLISHERS Ltd.

Publishers of Scarce Scholarly Books

NEW YORK. N. Y. 10012

1971

First Published 1892

HASKELL HOUSE PUBLISHERS Lᴛᴅ.
Publishers of Scarce Scholarly Books
280 LAFAYETTE STREET
NEW YORK, N. Y. 10012

Library of Congress Catalog Card Number: 76–116799

Standard Book Number 8383–1041–9

Printed in the United States of America

NOTE.

——◆——

My best thanks are due to Mr. W. R. Morfill, M.A., Reader in Russian and other Slavonic Languages in the University of Oxford, for advice as to the spelling of Polish names. When a name is familiar in a German or Latin form, e.g. Lemberg or Ladislas, that form has been generally adhered to; but, in the case of less-known names, an attempt has been made to give a more accurate representation of the Polish spelling.

CONTENTS.

INTRODUCTORY.

—••—

POLAND has been the scene of a struggle waged for more
than a thousand years between the influences of the East
and those of the West—a struggle which has profoundly
affected its religious no less than its political history.
Apparently it was a contest between the European and
the Asiatic; here the Tatars found the limits of their empire, and here was the bulwark of Europe against the Turk.
But underneath this conflict there lay the growing divergence
between the Slav of the East, disciplined by the Varangian,
corrupted by the Byzantine, rendered servile and barbarous
yet stimulated by the Tatar and the Slav of the West,
made warlike by the never-ending struggle with the German,
but unregulated by external domination or internal coercion.
As the danger from the Tatar passed away, the conflict
between the two branches of the Slavs assumed larger pro-
portions and a more bitter character. It was a contest
which united with the bitterness of political rivalry the gall
of religious hatred. To the enmity between the Slav of the
East and the Slav of the West was added the enmity between
the Church of the Patriarch and the Church of the Pope.
And when after the fall of Constantinople, Holy Moscow
stood in its place and became the metropolis not merely of
a nation but of a Church, the subjection of the Western
Slavs became to the Muscovite a part not merely of his
patriotism but of his religion.

B

The tide had not yet turned ; Poland, starting from the West, was adding to itself province after province that had once been ruled by Russians. It seemed that the hegemony of the Slavs was destined to rest with those of the West, not those of the East, and the Church of Rome to absorb that of Constantinople. The Reformation created a diversion in favour of the latter, and the religious duel in Poland became triangular, in which the latest comer seemed likely to be victorious. The introduction of the Jesuits again changed the aspect of affairs ; the Reformation in Poland was reduced to impotence, and Rome with its new ally turned again towards the schismatic Church. The struggle now lay between a power which derived its strength from a religious as well as a political sentiment of unity, and a power which depended on the one hand upon the undisciplined valour of some thousands of nobles, on the other hand upon an order marvellously adapted to the work of missionary propaganda. Poland became the most devotedly Catholic country in Europe, but its political independence was weakened and finally swept away. The success of the Catholic reaction and the intolerant aspect it assumed, acted like a powerful acid in splitting up Poland into its component parts ; at the same time the growth of a powerful Slav state in the East, and its assumption of the Panslavonic hegemony, exerted a magnetic attraction upon those elements of the Polish state whose bonds of cohesion had already been relaxed by the Catholic reaction. In Poland the Society of Jesus won its greatest success ; in Poland its success was fraught with the greatest risks to the welfare of the country.

CHAPTER I.

POLAND AND LITHUANIA BEFORE THE REFORMATION.

THE early history of Poland is wrapped in a darkness only illuminated by the fitful and misleading light of occasional legends about personages like Lech, after whom Early history the country was called Lechia; Cracus, who of Poland. founded Cracow; Popiel, who with his wife was devoured by rats; or Piast, who, miraculously called to the throne, founded the native dynasty called by that name [1]. During this legendary period anarchy rules supreme, till some leader delivers the country from external and internal enemies, and founds a dynasty which in its turn succumbs to anarchy, and is replaced by a new line of monarchs; and so on in an ever-recurring series till the reign of Mieczyslaw I opens an epoch of stabler rule and more reliable history. From the reign of his successor, Boleslas I, the real founder of Poland, dates the commencement of its growth from a petty duchy into the most powerful state in the East of Europe. This extension was carried on at the expense of Russia, whose internal struggles frequently led to Polish intervention; Casimir I and Boleslas II conquered Volhynia; in 1340 Red Russia was acquired, while Bohemia, Silesia, Pomerania, and even the Empire felt the power of the new kingdom. This growth was, however, Internal dis- crippled by the practice of dividing the country organisation. among the various sons of the monarchs as appanages;

---

[1] Connor, 'Letters on Poland.' Dunham's ' Hist. of Poland.'

their struggles left Poland at the mercy of the Tatars and
Teutonic knights, while the nobles began to regard the
monarchy as purely elective. The nascent but premature
union of the country was too weak to resist these disintegrating tendencies, and the 'dzielnica' or appanages became
easily separate, and developed each peculiar institutions of
its own [1]. Under Ladislas Lokotiek a fresh union was
brought about, not by gradual growth but all at once, and
Casimir the Great succeeded in some measure in restricting
the independence of these 'voivodies.' But scarcely had
this been accomplished when the Piast dynasty came to an
end, and Poland again found itself under the sway of an
oligarchy of nobles. When at last the royal power in the
person of Casimir IV broke the yoke of ecclesiastical and
secular oligarchy, which relying on the local independence
had held in check the power of the new dynasty, and summoned the lesser nobles to share in power, these latter
acquired their privileges as local assemblies of each voivodie,
which thereby gained fresh strength and began to discuss
the laws of the kingdom ; so that when the general Diet
was created, it was merely a union of delegates from each
voivodie, without being in any way a concentration of local
powers. The Diet possessed the shadow of sovereignty, the
substance remained with the dietines, and to them Casimir
himself appealed when he found the Diet refractory.

Both Diet and dietines were composed exclusively of
nobles or 'gentlemen'; there were practically only two

State of   classes of Poles, the nobles and peasants ;
Society.   there was no intermediate link. The towns
inhabited by German and Jew colonists were like 'oases'
in the desert, completely autonomous, living under Magde-
burg or Culm [2] law, sharing in no way in the life of the

---

[1] Nicolas Karéiev, 'Revue Historique,' 1891, pp. 241–288.

[2] The constitutions of these two cities served as models for the towns
in Poland, in much the same way as London did for the towns in
England.

country, and but nominally under the control of the king. Nevertheless, towards the close of the fifteenth century a process of 'polonisation' had begun in the towns ; but it was too late ; there was no strong monarchy to weld them into the national system. The nobles were in possession of the substance of power, and they used it exclusively in the interests of their own order to crush the growing privileges of the towns, to restrict the higher offices in the Church to nobles, and to render their authority more than ever absolute over their ' subjects.' The nobles and the constitution became identical ; for their sake only did Poland exist.

The history of Lithuania presents a somewhat similar development. Originally the Poles and the Russians belonged to the same race ; it was their development that turned them into different and Lithuania. hostile nationalities. ' The Slav moulded by the Liakhi, converted to the Church of Rome and subject to the influences of the West, became the Pole ; the Slav moulded by the Variagi, converted to the Greek Church and subject to Byzantine influences, became the Russian[1].' The borderland between these two nationalities took its name from the Turanian races against which the Slavs had early to contend—the Semigals, Ingrians, Esthonians, Livonians, and Lithuanians. Most of the territory afterwards called Lithuania was united with Russia under the Varangian princes St. Vladimir and Iaroslav the Great, whose empire centred round the glory of Kiev. But here, as in Poland, premature union gave way to anarchy, due to the practice of dividing the land among the sons of its monarchs, and the confusion of ideas about hereditary right[2]. During this period Russia, or Ruthenia, split up into a number of small

[1] Rambaud, 'History of Russia.'
[2] Joachim Lelewel, ' Histoire de la Lithuanie et de la Ruthenie jusqu'à 1569.'

states ; while in the North democratic elements became
prominent in a group of great cities like Novgorod, Pskov,
and Viatka, resembling the republics of Italy or the Hansa
towns of North Germany[1], and the monarchical elements
gathered towards the East round Vladimir and Moscow,
a colony established by Dolgorouki, the aristocratic elements gravitated towards Poland in the West. Then for
two centuries Russia lay crushed under the heel of the
Tatar, till the Grand Dukes of Moscow, relying on their
support, then emancipating themselves from this control,
made themselves gradually masters of most of Russia that
had not been absorbed in Poland or the Lithuanian Empire,
and claimed as the representatives of St. Vladimir the hegemony of the Slavonic race. Meanwhile Mindvog and Ge-
dimin were extending the sway of Lithuania over the south-
west as far as Kiev, when in 1380 Jagiello became king of
Union with   Poland.   Lithuania retained its separate exist-
Poland.   ence as a Grand Duchy, but its provinces
gradually became Polish ; the peasants sank into a position
no better than those in Poland[2]; the nobles assumed the
manners and language of the Polish aristocracy, and from
1564 to 1566 acquired all their privileges ; two chambers
were created on the Polish model, and Sigismund renounced
his hereditary claim to the Grand Duchy, so that it became
elective like Poland, and the way was paved for the union
of the two states into a homogeneous whole at Lublin in
1569. 'This complete state plays the same part in Russian
history as the Burgundy of Philip the Good and Charles
the Bold in that of France.   Made up in a great degree of
Russian as well as Polish and Lithuanian elements, it was
many times on the point of annihilating Russia in the same
way as Burgundy, composed of French, Batavian, and

---

[1] Novgorod was a member of this league.

[2] Lelewel; this historian is very bitter against the Russians, whom he
maintains to be nothing but Tatars.

German provinces, had been on the point of annihilating the French nation[1].'

The religious history of the two branches of the Slavs was not the least of the causes which engendered the national antipathy between them. Christianity is said to have been introduced into Poland by Mieczyslaw I [2], under the influence of his wife Dombrowka, daughter of the King of Hungary, to whom also is attributed the founding of seven sees, with the archbishoprics of Gnesen and Cracow. There are, however, traces of it in Poland as early as the seventh century, when Poland formed part of the great Slavonic State which was converted by Cyril and Methodius [3], who are credited with the invention of the Slavonic alphabet and translation of the Bible [4]. From its origin, the Polish Church hung somewhat loosely upon Rome. The Pontiffs were compelled to sanction many variations in it derived from the Eastern Church, by the fear that any attempt to enforce a more uniform system would lead to its complete transference to the Church of Constantinople. An additional element of disturbance consisted of the policy of the German missionaries, who held most of the livings in Poland and occupied all the religious houses, which they utilised as a basis for political propaganda. After the complete separation of the Eastern and Western Churches, the Popes made a determined effort to render the Polish Church once for all dependent, and Methodius was declared a heretic ; this attempt, though strenuously supported by the German ecclesiastics, met with little success, and the Church long retained some of the characteristics of an independent National Church. This independence is conspicuously illustrated by the career of Stanislas Szczepanowski [5], whose

Religious history.

Independence of Rome.

---

[1] Rambaud.
[2] Andreas Wengerscius, 'Slav. Reformata,' Amst. 1679.
[3] Krasinski.   [4] Wengerscius.
[5] Wengerscius, p. 11 ; Krasinski, ' Ref. in Poland.'

struggle with Boleslas II is closely parallel with that between
Beket and Henry II. His death was probably due to a
judicial decree, and the king was certainly supported by a
considerable party, although a combination of the clerical
and aristocratic factions drove him into exile. The triumph
of the Church did not produce any great change in the
relations between the temporal and spiritual powers, and
Ladislas Spindleshanks was able to restrict the independence of the clergy, and defying Rome, to decide the question
of tithes in favour of the temporal power. Services were
performed mostly in the national tongue; priests were
married up to a very late date; and the kings maintained
their claim to nominate bishops. There was, however,
little dispute about doctrine : the sects which appeared in
Poland, such as the Waldenses, Flagellants, and Fraticelli,
were of foreign origin, and gained little ground in Poland ;
but feeling against Rome, kept alive by hostility to its
German emissaries, was further embittered by the encroachments of the Teutonic knights. Thus, when
in the fourteenth and fifteenth centuries the
idea of a Universal Church began to give way before the
movement for National Churches, seen alike in the career of
Wiclif and the liberties of the Gallican Church, it was but
natural that the preaching of Huss should find an echo in
Poland [1]. In 1341 John Pirnensis had preached that the
Pope was Anti-Christ, and had made some followers, who
were afterwards absorbed in the Hussites. Polish youths
were in the habit of going to Prague to be educated, and it
was Hieronymus, one of Huss' fellow-workers, who organized
the University of Cracow. In 1420 the Bohemians offered
the crown to Jagiello on certain conditions, but that
monarch was already burdened with a war against the
Teutonic knights, and was unwilling to become involved
in another with the Emperor, while he saw that the dissen-

Influence of Huss.

[1] Wengerscius, pp. 23–25, 114, 115.

sions between the Taborites[1] and Calixtines would render his crown in Bohemia very insecure. In 1427 there was a conference between Roman Catholics and Hussites at Cracow, but it led to no accommodation, and the latter began a revolutionary movement in Poland which soon ended in failure. The suppression of the Hussites did not, however, crush out all religious independence, and in 1459 John Ostrorog submitted to the Diet an important project of reform, in which he renounced the supremacy of the Pope, maintained that the clergy should bear public burdens equally with other citizens, and protested against annates, appeals to Rome, and indulgences. In 1500 the nobility of Great Poland, assembled at Posen demanded the concession of the communion in both kinds, to the laity as well as the clergy[2]. Some elements of religious independence were thus maintained up to the very eve of the Reformation, and contributed not a little to the ready acceptance with which its doctrines met in Poland.

While the Slavs of the West gave a dubious adhesion to the Church of Rome, those of the East submitted definitely to the Greek Church. They had constantly been brought into contact with Greek Christianity by the expeditions under Varangian princes against the Eastern Empire, but that religion, despite the conversions of Olga and Askold, does not seem to have made much progress in Russia till Vladimir, the Russian Clovis, after instituting a search for the best religion, chose that of Byzantium. The choice of a Church which put forth no pretensions to governing the State saved Russia from struggles between the secular, a national power, and the spiritual, a foreign power; but it excluded Russia from Western Europe, and separated it

Religious history of the Greek Church.

---

[1] Wengerscius, pp. 181, 182.
[2] Ibid. p. 73. Krasinski's 'Ref. in Poland' is mainly based on Wengerscius.

from the religion of the rest of the Slavs, inflamed its rivalry with Poland, and deprived it of much influence over the neighbouring Slavs. The metropolitan of the Russian Church was established at Kiev, 'the city of four hundred churches,' whose splendour, according to Adam of Bremen, rivalled that of Constantinople : the church of Novgorod, with its archbishop, was practically independent. After the destruction of Kiev by Bogoliubski, and afterwards by the Tatars, the metropolitans transferred their seat to Vladimir, and then to Moscow, whence they extended their spirtiual sway side by side with the secular power of the Grand Union of   Dukes. In 1438, at the Council of Florence, 1438.   a union of the Greek and Latin Churches was brought about by the metropolitan Isidor, who was made a cardinal ; but on his return his compromise was rejected with indignation, and he was deposed and thrown into prison. In Lithuania paganism survived till the personal union with Poland in 1380, when the Greek Church became predominant. It was scarcely natural that this Church should remain under the jurisdiction of a metropolitan residing in the capital of its great rival, and in 1415 Vitold caused the election of an archbishop of Kiev, independent of the metropolitan at Moscow : the Church of Halich, united with Poland in 1340, recognised him as its metropolitan, and a complete separation took place from the Church of Russia. Until 1453 both were dependent upon the Patriarch of Constantinople, but after that the Church of Russia became absolutely independent. Thus at the time of the Reformation there existed in Lithuania, the Roman Catholics, the Uniates or members of the Greek Church who recognised the union of 1438, those members forming the great majority who regarded the metropolitan of Kiev as the head of their Church under the Patriarch, and finally, considerable numbers of the peasantry who still clung to paganism.

CHAPTER II.

THE REFORMATION IN POLAND[1].

THE history of the Reformation in Poland was largely affected by the peculiar character of the country; the Lutheran confession was naturally the one accepted by the towns which were chiefly composed of German inhabitants; but the national enmity between Slavs and Germans retarded its acceptance by the Polish inhabitants, and it was the Helvetian Church which spread most widely among them. The Bohemian Brethren[2] grew to considerable importance; but what principally characterised the Reformation in Poland was the influence to which the Anti-Trinitarian sect, called after the two Socini, attained. Lutheranism appeared in Poland very soon, and in 1518 a monk, Thomas Knade of Dantzic, married, and began to preach against Rome: many of the inhabitants became Protestants. In 1523 Sigismund I ordered the town council to maintain the existing religion, while the archbishop of Gnesen went there to stop the progress of heresy. His failure was followed in 1525 by an attack upon the town council, which the citizens replaced by one consisting exclusively of Protestants. Sigismund temporised till he had made peace with Albert

The Reformation in Poland.

Lutheranism.

---

[1] The chief authorities are Krasinski's two books and Wengerscius. D'Aubigné also gives an account of the Reformation in Poland. There is a short description in 'Respublica sive status Regni Poloniae,' Lugd. 1627, but it is not of much value. The monumental work of Thuanus is of course the basis of most modern books on the subject.

[2] Wengerscius.

of Brandenburg, and then, acting probably more from
political than religious motives, succeeded in suppressing it.
The reaction spread to Elbing, Thorn, and Braunsberg.
Masovia [1] took strong measures against the Reformation,
and it never spread much in that province. Students were
forbidden to frequent foreign universities, but this, like so
many other ordinances, remained a dead letter; for in 1549
there was a riot at Cracow, and the students being dis-
satisfied with the authorities of the University, went abroad
in great numbers to Goldberg and Könisberg, whence they
returned imbued with Protestant doctrines. In 1534 the
Reformation made a fresh start, and a Lutheran Church
was opened on the estates of Gorka in Great Poland, which
had been much affected by Hussite doctrines : soon it
spread again into Polish Prussia, despite the efforts of
Hosen, bishop of Ermeland, and into Livonia, which submitted to Poland in 1561, and where the German population had followed the conquests of the Teutonic knights
and Order of the Sword.

The strength of the Bohemian Church lay among the
nobles, who began to join this Church [2] soon after the
Bohemian   arrival of the Brethren in 1548, when they
Church.   were received by Andreas Gorka, Castellan of
Posen. A church was built by subscription at Cracow ;
aided by national sympathies they gained many adherents
among the nobles of Great Poland, and in 1555 they
established a union with the Helvetian Church of Poland
at the Synod of Kozminek. The latter Church predominated
in Lithuania and southern Poland, most of the principal
families belonging to it. Despite these successes, the cause
of the Reformation was seriously hampered by bitter dissensions between the Lutherans and other Protestants, who
appeared to hate each other more than they hated Rome.

---

[1] 'Respublica sive status Reg. Pol.' p. 115.
[2] Wengerscius, pp. 81–90.

These quarrels induced many influential families which were inclined to accept the new doctrines, to return to the Roman Church merely for the sake of peace and security. Another cause of hindrance was the spread of Socinianism. Anti-Trinitarian doctrines which alarmed many, and frightened them back into the orthodox Church. Before the death of Sigismund I, a society had been formed at Cracow which entered into bold discussions on theological matters. Most of its members subsequently returned to the Roman Church, but it was here that Pastoris, by attacking the doctrine of the Trinity, laid the foundations of that sect which was subsequently called after Lelio and Faustus Socinus. Stancari and Lismanini became the pioneers of this sect. In 1551 Lelio Socinus visited Poland, and Gonesius publicly proclaimed Socinian doctrines at a synod held in 1556 under the patronage of John Kiszka. The Protestants on Calvin's advice made efforts to suppress them, and in 1564 all ministers from abroad denying the mystery of the Trinity were ordered to leave the country. This produced little effect. Blandrata and Pauli[1] developed these doctrines, and at the synod of Wengrow in 1565 their Church received a definite organisation. One of their most eminent members, Budny, made an accurate translation of the Bible, and Smalcius composed a Socinian catechism called the 'Catechesis Ecclesiarum in regno Poloniae,' which was condemned by the English Parliament as ' blasphemous, erroneous, and scandalous.' Their rules of morality were very strict, but they maintained the doctrine of passive obedience, and condemned the resistance of the Dutch and Huguenots. A school was established at Rakow[2], which became famous, and produced many scholars and authors ; their congregations, however, remained small, and were composed chiefly of wealthy landowners.

[1] Wengerscius, p. 85.   [2] Ibid. p. 90.

The influence of the Reformation soon made itself felt in national policy and legislation. Whether from lack of conviction or lack of power Sigismund Augustus pursued a dubious course; but the Diet began to evince a considerable hostility towards the Church of Rome. In 1550 it was decided that no one but the king had the right of judging citizens or of condemning them to any penalty whatever. In 1552 the clergy were allowed to retain the right to judge heresy, but without any power of inflicting civil or criminal penalties on the condemned; and a proposition was brought forward to deprive the bishops of their seats in the senate, but it was not carried. The Diet made considerable demands[1] on the Council of Trent; these included (1) that Mass should be performed in the national language, (2) Communion in both kinds, (3) marriage of priests, (4) abolition of annates, (5) convocation of a national council. The idea of creating a National Church in Poland somewhat similar to that of England, met with considerable acceptance at this time; and the hope of accomplishing this object without violently breaking with Roman Catholic doctrine prevented many from openly joining the Protestants. The Roman Catholics, conscious of their weakness, were not opposed to the idea of a national council, and on the other hand it was approved of by John à Lasco[2], the most celebrated of Polish reformers.

John of Lask was born in 1499; his education had been entirely entrusted to his uncle the archbishop of Gnesen, who had taken him to the Lateran Council and left him to study at Bologna and Rome, intending that he should succeed to his high position in the Church. With this aim he made him dean of Cracow.

Influence on the Diet. (side note)

John à Lasco. (side note)

---

[1] Wengerscius, p. 78; also Krasinski, 'Religious Hist.' and 'Ref. in Poland.'

[2] Herman Dalton, 'John à Lasco.' This book unfortunately only deals with Laski's early life till his return from England.

John, however, on his travels met Erasmus, with whom he lived at Basle, and other eminent Humanists. At Paris he became acquainted with Marguerite of Valois, and on his return to Basle fell in with Zwingli, Rhenanus, and Auerbach. Deep study of their works gradually unsettled his faith in the Roman Church, but his open secession was retarded by respect for his uncle, and the hope that the Church would reform itself from within. After some hesitation he made up his mind to definitely embrace the Reformation, and left Poland for Louvain, whence he was compelled to flee before the rigorous measures of Charles V. He found refuge in Emden, where the Frieslanders had accepted the Reformation, but refused to submit to the emissaries of Luther. Here, after much trouble with the monks, Anabaptists, and Lutherans, he succeeded in organising the Frisian Church. The Countess Anne, though a Protestant, did not feel strong enough to support him after the promulgation of the Interim, and Laski accepted an invitation to England, where with Cranmer and Peter Martyr he joined in the work of establishing Protestant doctrines. After a second visit to Emden he returned to England, whence he was driven by the Catholic reaction under Mary. He arrived in Poland in 1556, and was entrusted with the superintendence of the Reformed Churches in Little Poland. He also had an active share in the famous Bible of Radziwill [1], and published several works, which were, however, destroyed by the Jesuits.

However much the Roman Catholics in Poland might approve of the idea of a national council, it was in the last degree distasteful to the authorities at Rome, and the efforts of Lippomani who visited Poland in 1558, of the legate Commendoni, Efforts of the Roman Catholics.

---

[1] This famous Bible was published at Brześć in 1563. There is a copy in the Bodleian, but it is extremely rare, two copies only being in existence. The sons of Radziwill all turned Catholics, and signalised their conversion by burning all their father's heretical books.

and the Jesuit Canisius, provincial of Upper Germany, were all directed towards reanimating those who were still faithful to Rome. They succeeded in finally winning back Orzechowski, who had embraced the reformed doctrines, not so much from love of truth as because they suited his violent temper[1], and had repeatedly changed sides, always signalising each tergiversation by fresh abuse of his former associates. But the soul of the Catholic cause was Stanislas Hosen, cardinal and bishop of Ermeland. In this latter capacity he had vainly tried to stop the spread of Lutheran

Hosen.   doctrines in Polish Prussia. Born in 1504 at Cracow, Hosen[2] was educated at Padua, where he became the friend of Cardinal Pole, and at Bologna, whence he returned to Poland, and was made successively bishop of Cracow and of Ermeland. Bayle calls him the greatest man Poland ever produced; but though a man of stainless character and great culture, he was actuated by the bitterest animosity against the Protestants, and is credited with the opinions that faith should not be kept with heretics, that it was necessary to confute them not by argument but by the authority of the magistrate, and that it was better to abandon the realm to the Muscovites than to them. In 1561 he was made President of the Council of Trent, and was distinguished by his uncompromising advocacy of the most extravagant claims of Rome. He became grand penitentiary of the Church, and died at Rome in 1579, having spent his last years there. It was owing to his zeal and activity that the Church of Rome in Poland was not utterly overwhelmed. At the provincial synod of Piotrkow[3] in 1551, he was invited to draw up a confession of faith, which was to serve as a test of orthodoxy; and this con-

---

[1] Krasinski. Wengerscius, pp. 80, 210.
[2] 'Stan. Hosii Vita,' Stanislas Rescio auctore, Romae, 1587.
[3] Preface to the 'Opera Stan. Hosii,' Antwerp, 1571. This edition is very incomplete, and does not contain his important letters on the state of heresy and summoning the Jesuits.

fession subsequently received the official approval of the Church of Rome. It was here resolved to extirpate heresy by all possible means [1]; but this only provoked the resolutions of the Diet of 1552. In 1556 the papal envoy Lippomani induced the synod of Lowicz to pass many resolutions against heresy, but the attempt to re-establish ecclesiastical jurisdiction in such matters failed; a similar attempt in a case of sacrilege ended in the burning of a woman and some Jews, who were condemned on the absurd charge of selling the host. The influence of Canisius induced the Diet of Piotrkow to maintain its allegiance to Rome, and Sigismund to refuse all modification of episcopal rights, while Commendoni prevented the summoning of a national council, and fanned the dissensions between the various Protestant Churches. In spite of all this the Reformation was gaining ground in Poland. Skarga declared that two thousand Roman Catholic churches had been converted to Protestant uses ; while the clergy and the court were mutually accusing each other of cowardice and negligence with regard to the heretics, a project, of which *Union of* John à Lasco had not lived to see the con- *Sandomir.* summation, the union of the Protestant Churches, was at length completed at Sandomir in 1570. Thus Lutherans and Calvinists could face the Roman Catholics with a united front, and even the Socinians, who had been excluded from the 'consensus Sandomiriensis,' were rapidly on the increase, till it was said—

> 'Tota jacet Babylon; destruxit tecta Lutherus,
> Calvinus muros, sed fundamenta Socinus.'

The Church of Rome in Poland was indeed shaken from roof to foundation ; its stoutest adherents had lost heart. Poland was slowly but surely following in the *State of the* wake of the other northern countries of Europe *Reformation.* —of England, Denmark, North Germany, Holland, Sweden

---

[1] Wengerscius, pp. 207 sq., 222 sq.

and Norway—and breaking away from the yoke of Rome. The critical moment had come ; the balance hung trembling ; the Reformation had already begun to preponderate when Stanislas Hosen, the greatest of Poland's prelates, to whom Rome already owed so much, cast into the scale of Catholicism that 'sword whose hilt was at Rome, whose point was everywhere'—the Society of Jesus. It was a step the full effects of which were not seen till almost every vestige of the Reformation had been washed out by the wave of reaction, and Catholicism was established in Poland as it had never been established before. The introduction of the Jesuits was not merely an episode in the history of Catholicism in Poland ; it was not merely the recovery by Rome of a country that was falling away from its influence ; there was Catholicism in Poland before the introduction of the Jesuits, and there was Catholicism after, but they were not the same thing. Whatever be the merits of the Protestant and Catholic Churches as religious ideals, Protestantism has at least been invaluable as an intellectual stimulus, and no country was ever in more urgent need of an intellectual stimulus than Poland ; the want of this stimulus working with other causes produced an effect that can be paralleled not even in Portugal, and the history of Poland from the last quarter of the sixteenth century, political, intellectual, social, religious, may be summed up in this one word—reaction.

CHAPTER III.

BEGINNINGS OF THE JESUITS IN POLAND.

WHILE the movement for reform which the Renascence called forth, took in Germany the form of separation from Rome and abolition of some of its fundamental institutions, such as the monastic orders, in Italy it confined itself to a reformation within the pale of the Church, and a regeneration of the monastic system which had been so potent a support to the Church of Rome. This movement was seen in the foundation of new orders like the Capuchins, Barnabites, and Theatins, which, emancipating themselves from many of the regulations that had hampered the older monastic orders, devoted themselves more especially to active work, to preaching, confessing, attending the sick and converting heretics. Aiming like the Protestant movement at reform, they sought it by diametrically opposite means, by renovating not abolishing the old order, by reaction not by revolution. Of this movement the master-type was the Society of Jesus.

This new order owed its foundation to a Spanish soldier of fortune, Don Iñigo Lopez de Recalde, who, cut off from a soldier's career by a wound received before Pampeluna, devoted himself to religion. His The Society of Jesus. visions at Mount Montserrat, in the cave at Manresa, in the cell of St. Barbara, illustrate the enthusiastic and mystical, as the 'Spiritual Exercises' and 'Constitutions' do the practical side of his mind. He set to work to complete his neglected education, and at Paris won over Faber, Xavier, Salmeron, Lainez, and Bobadilla, who all took the vow of chastity and swore to spend their lives at Jerusalem, devoted in absolute poverty to the care of the Christians or conversion of the Saracens; if this were impossible they were to offer themselves unconditionally to the service of the Pope. The Turks prevented their original intention, and after many difficulties at Rome, the Pope sanctioned conditionally in 1540 and unreservedly in 1543 the establishment of the Society of Jesus, and Loyola was elected first general. Its ostensible object was the conversion of the heathen, but while Xavier went to the East and the Jesuits spread into every quarter of the globe, the centre of their activity was in Europe, where they devoted themselves to the re-establishment of the tottering Papacy. Not only did they reject the monastic habit, but they disregarded the common devotional exercises, and set three main objects before them—preaching, confessing, and education of the young.

The Society spread rapidly in Italy, Spain, and Portugal, more slowly in France, the Netherlands, and Germany, where its success seemed for some time doubtful. First Jesuits in Poland. Here there were two Provinces, and it was Peter Canisius, Provincial of Upper Germany, who first of the Jesuits penetrated into Poland. Rumours had reached the Pope of a Diet to be held at Piotrkow in 1558, where religion was to be the chief subject of discussion. Justly alarmed at the imminent prospect of the secession of Poland, he sent Mentuatus as legate to the Diet, accompanied by Canisius [1]. The Jesuit lost no opportunities of preaching and furthering the interests of Rome by all possible means [2]; he pointed out the evils of the mutual accusations which the clergy and court brought against each other; the king, who constantly refused to persecute [3], was encouraged to

[1] Sacchinus, ' Hist. Soc. Jesu,' ii. 52.   [2] Ibid. ii. 121.
[3] Sacchinus, ii. 121, 122; Crétineau-Joly, i 459. The latter historian

refuse any modification of episcopal rights, and the Diet was induced to prohibit all innovation. The visit of Canisius did not lead at once to any further steps on the part of the Jesuits, but Polish youths began to visit their school at Vienna, and among them Stanislas Kostka [1], who led a saintly life, and was canonised after his death. He became acquainted with Canisius, and on his departure from Vienna proceeded to Rome, where he met Warszewski, afterwards high in the favour of Sigismund III, and Aloysius Gonzaga; here he died in 1568 at the age of eighteen. The Poles paid great veneration to his name: he was claimed as the Patron of Poland, and legends grew up that his appearance at Chocim gave the victory to the Poles, and rescued Przemysl from the Cossacks [2]. It was in 1564 [3] that Hosen wrote to Lainez asking for some members of the Society. The General dispatched some from Rome and others from Lower Germany, with Christopher Strombelius as leader. Their journey was beset with hardships; they could enter neither city nor village because of the plague, and slept in the open air.

Kostka.

On their arrival Hosen located them in a vacant monastery which had once belonged to the Franciscans at Braunsberg, near Frauenberg [4], where he had his episcopal seat, and they received material help from the canons [5]. Their arrival was also welcomed by Commendoni, the papal legate, who attached one of them,

Introduction of the Jesuits.

---

of the Socie'y is valueless as far as Poland is concerned: the early part is merely a translation of Sacchinus; he sometimes quotes Ranke with approval, but it is from the garbled French edition which was justly branded by Macaulay.

[1] 'St. Stan. Kostka Vita.' Sacchinus.

[2] 'Life of St. Kostka' (Library of Religious Thought).

[3] Sacchinus. Ranke has a statement (vol. ii. p. 56. Mrs. Austin's transl.) that the first members arrived in 1570. This must refer to the college at Wilna, but it is not quite clear.

[4] 'Sive Warmiam ubi sedem episcopus et collegium canonicorum habet.' Sacchinus.

[5] 'Annuae Litterae Soc. Jesu,' 1586, 1587.

Balthazar Hostovinus[1], to himself, and took him on his visitations to aid in the foundation of colleges. Andreas Noskowski[2], bishop of Pultusk, was induced to found a college in that city. In 1566 Canisius made a second visit to Poland, and induced Valerian, bishop of Wilna[3], who was well stricken in years, to signalise his last days by the establishment of a Jesuit college[4]. In 1567 an attempt was made to introduce the Society into Elbing, but without success. The settlement at Braunsberg was more prosperous, and in 1569 it was converted into a regular college. A fourth college was founded at Posen, 1571, by its bishop, Adam Konarski[5], who persuaded the authorities of the city to give them one of its principal churches with two hospitals and a school, while he endowed them with an estate and made them a present of his library[6]. Sigismund viewed these proceedings with indifference if not with approbation. He had been dissuaded from his project of divorcing his wife, Barbara Radziwill, which the Protestants advocated, by Maggio, who had succeeded Canisius as Provincial of Upper Germany. The Jesuits[7] produced a favourable impression on him, and at his death in 1572 he bequeathed the Royal Library to the Society[8]. Uchanski, who had been one of those who freely discussed theological subjects at Cracow University, now became one of the foremost patrons of the order, and his example was followed by many of the bishops, who relied more on the zeal of the new order than on the efforts of the local clergy.

The immediate result of this success was to stimulate the

---

[1] Sacchinus, viii. 113.

[2] Johannes Argentus, 'Liber ad Sig. de Rebus Soc. Jesu in Regno Pol.' Ingolstadt, 1616.

[3] Ibid., also Ranke and Guettée, 'Hist. Soc. Jesu.'   [4] Ranke.

[5] Argentus.   [6] Krasinski.

[7] Guettée, one of the historians of the Society, asserts that Alphonse de Carillo became confessor to Sigismund II; but this is only another instance of the inaccuracy of historians in regard to Poland. The Sigismund to whom Carillo was confessor was Prince of Transylvania, Stephen Batory's son.   [8] Argentus, p. 224.

Protestants to fresh measures of defence against Rome. At the election Diet of Warsaw in 1573, a resolution [1] was carried to the effect that no one should be injured or persecuted on account of his religion. From that time the kings of Poland took an oath to maintain this resolution. In 1579 the payment of tithes to the clergy was entirely suspended, and the papal nuncio asserts that by this act alone twelve hundred parish priests were left wholly destitute. At the same time a supreme court of judicature composed of laity and clergy was established, which decided all cases ecclesiastical as well as temporal. There can be little doubt that if the Protestants had acted at all unanimously they would have been irresistible, and by electing a king of their own belief could have permanently established the Reformation in Poland. But this unanimity was the one thing lacking; while their chief opponent was the Society of Jesus—an instrument wielded with unerring skill and precision, obeying one will and actuated by one impulse—the Protestants turned their arms against one another in the face of the enemy. Before the Union of Sandomir the Lutherans had declared that it was better to join the Jesuits than the Bohemians, and that union was never much more than a hollow mockery. Not only were the various sects independent and hostile, but the Churches of the various provinces of each sect had no common organisation; while their opponents were a regular trained army, they depended upon the isolated endeavours of individuals or irregular bands. Though they probably at this time outnumbered the Roman Catholics, they were unable to place a chief of their own upon the throne. Their

[1] It is said by Krasinski that this resolution was proposed by the bishop of Cujavia, Karnkowski, as a measure of self-defence : the Diet readily accepted it but Commendoni subsequently induced them all to protest, except Francis Krasinski, bishop of Cracow. The dignities and privileges of the Roman Catholic bishops were guaranteed, but the obligation of church patrons to bestow benefices exclusively on Catholics was abolished. ' Rel. Hist. of Slavs,' pp. 176, 77.

Measures of the Protestants.

leader was John Firley ; but he was a Helvetian, and rather
than further his election the Lutherans, who were led by
Zebrzdowski, declared for the Roman Catholic candidate,
the Archduke Ernest.   Commendoni had already begun to
intrigue for his succession before the death of Sigismund,
but the emperor refused the Legate's request for men and

Election   money to overawe the Diet, and the mistakes of
of a king.   the Austrian envoys made this scheme fail.
The election ultimately ended in favour of Henry of Anjou,
who seems originally to have been put forward by Coligny
and the Huguenots, who meditated a grand Protestant
League against Rome and Austria.   St. Bartholomew almost
ruined his chances, and it was only after he had repeatedly
sworn to observe the rights of the Protestants that Firley
placed the crown upon his head.   Hosen had protested
against this oath, representing the decree of January, 1573, as
treason to God, while Solikowski advised Henry to swear all
that was required of him, because he would have ample
opportunity to restore Catholicism after his election.

CHAPTER IV.

Progress of the Society under Stephen Batory.

A few months after his accession to the throne of Poland, Henry of Anjou precipitately fled, to secure the French crown which devolved upon him after the death of his brother Charles IX. The Diet waited a year for his return, and then elected Stephen Batory, Prince of Conversion of Transylvania and a Protestant, on condition of Batory. his marrying Anna, the last of the Jagiellonian line. The Roman Catholics were however equal to the occasion, and Solikowski, the only one of their faith who accompanied the delegates to announce his election, succeeded, in spite of their vigilance, in gaining a private interview with Batory, in which he managed to persuade that prince that the only chance he had of maintaining himself on the throne was to embrace Catholicism. This was indeed the most prudent course he could pursue, for though the Protestants in Poland outnumbered the Roman Catholics, yet the latter were by far the strongest sect in Poland and afforded the firmest basis of support; moreover, he would have the external support of the Pope, if not of Austria, while Anna would never be brought to marry a Protestant. Further, he had never been very hostile to Rome, and before his conversion had summoned the Jesuits into Transylvania [1]. This was an important point gained by the Romanists, for though Batory declined to follow the advice of Bolognetto [2] to

---

[1] Sacchinus.　　　　[2] Ranke, 'Hist. of the Popes.'

restrict his favours to zealous Catholics, and though he
bestowed churches on the Protestants and checked persecution, it was during his reign and through the liberality of him
and his wife, that the Society of Jesus took firm root in
His favours to Poland. He became a great patron of the
the Jesuits. Jesuits, who called him ' pater et patronus
noster[1].' He summoned Stanislas Socolovius[2], a prominent
member of the order in Poland and author of several contro-
versial works, to his court, and employed him on business of
every description[3] ; he called him his ' eye,' and took him as
a companion to his camp at Marienberg[4], Grodno, &c.,
while the Jesuit made the best use of his opportunities by
preaching and converting heretics, schismatics, Jews, and
Tatars[5]. To Batory's liberality, which 'they can never'
sufficiently praise[6],' the Jesuits owed their establishments at
Riga, Dorpat, and Polock[7], the University at Wilna, besides
residences at Waradin, Alba Julia[8], and Claudiopolis[9],
where a University was established. Their colleges were
exempted from all imposts, and Batory, lest the State should
suffer, made up the amount from his own purse. He professed his unique affection for the Society because of its
services to the Church of God, and declared its encouragement ' to be the only means of promoting the cause of
Catholicism, and restoring to health minds that had been
corrupted with heresy[10].' His wife was no less zealous in
the cause, and the colleges of Pultusk and Lublin experi-

---

[1] ' Annuae Litterae,' 1586, 87.   [2] Thuanus, pars iii, 494 D.
[3] ' Annuae Litterae,' 1585.
[4] It is uncertain whether this is the town in Polish Prussia or in
Livonia ; most of Batory's wars were against Muscovy, but at one time
he established a camp in Polish Prussia, to guard against Swedish in-
vasion.   [5] ' Ann. Litt.' 1585.   [6] Ibid. ; also Argentus, p. 224.
[7] The Jesuits are not very consistent about the spelling of this name,
but a remark of Piasecius, 'Chronica gestorum in Eur.' p. 6, shows that
this college was at Polock in Lithuania, not Plock in Masovia.
[8] Weissemberg.
[9] Klausenburg ; both these were of course in Transylvania, a part of
the Jesuit Province.   [10] Argentus, chap. v.

enced her generosity [1]; the example of the king and queen was followed by the nobles, many of whom were beginning to return to the Catholic Church. Chodkiewicz, Hetman of Lithuania, who had been converted by Stanislas Warszewicz[2] described the Society as ' labouring in every corner of the globe to instruct youth, extirpate heresy, and correct evil habits,' and, convinced that ' its success would be beneficial to the Republic [3],' founded a college at Kroze in the palatinate of Wilna for the education of the sons of nobles. A gentleman of the king's bedchamber gave them a chapel at Wilna[4], and the Society acquired the chief families in the land as its patrons.

It was under such favourable auspices as these that the Jesuits commenced their arduous task in Po- Spread of the land ; so great was their success, that at the end Society. of Batory's reign the members of the Society numbered over three hundred and sixty, possessing twelve colleges, besides residences and missions [5]. From Braunsberg, Pultusk, Wilna, and Posen, the four centres which the Society possessed at the commencement of the reign, it spread into almost every corner of Poland and Lithuania. In Polish Prussia, which was deeply imbued Polish Prussia. with Lutheranism, their progress was naturally slow, and Braunsberg long remained their only establishment in that province. An attempt had been made to introduce the Jesuits into Elbing, but the population had shown such a marked hostility that it was reluctantly abandoned. It was not until 1586 that the Society obtained a foothold in

---

[1] 'Annuae Litterae,' 1585.   [2] Argentus, chap. v.
[3] Ibid.   [4] Ibid.
[5] 'Annuae Litterae,' 1585. The only Annual Letters in the Bodleian are for the years 1585–87 and 1600 ; this is unfortunate, for though the Letters are the most uninviting reading possible, and full of the absurdest fables, they are useful for statistics as to numbers and details about the founders of various colleges. The account of Argentus is useful ; he was visitor of the Province for some years. These figures include Transylvania.

another Prussian town by the Mission to Dantzic [1].   Masovia

Masovia.   had never been much affected by the Reformation ; there was consequently less need for the
Jesuits, and no fresh college was established besides that of
Pultusk till the middle of Sigismund III's reign, when the
bishop of Camenz founded one at Lomza on the Narew [2].

Great Poland.   In Great Poland two colleges were started, one
by Konarski at Posen, in the reign of Sigismund
II, the other at Kalisz by Karnkowski, archbishop of Gnesen,
in 1584 [3].   At Posen the Society seems to have been very
successful, in spite of the plague which thinned its numbers ;
many townspeople and several nobles had been won over,
and a hundred and thirty conversions were made, including

Little Poland.   thirty German Protestants, in one year [4].   In
Little Poland a college was founded at Lublin,
which received considerable aid from the queen and Senate
of Poland, and the Society was very active at Cracow, where
there were two establishments, one for ' professed ' members,
who could only live on alms, and another for novices.   A
noble lady had granted them two rich estates, and a church
had been built for their use.   Here they held four separate
services on Sundays, when their preaching made many
converts.   Nothing came amiss to their zeal ; they formed
associations to look after the sick; they supplied help to
those whom disease or shame prevented from seeking it ;
they paid the debts of many, and relieved families reduced

Red Russia.   to the utmost misery.   In Red Russia a college
was established at Jaroslav and a mission at
Lemberg [5], which, besides being the seat of a Roman Catholic archbishop, was also that of a Russian and Armenian
bishop [6].   Here they were supported by the Castellan, and
though there were only three members, they made excursions

---

[1] Gedanum is the pseudo-classical name used by the Jesuits.
[2] Argentus.   [3] ' Ann. Litt.'   [4] Ibid.
[5] Lwow in Polish, Leopolis in pseudo-classical Latin.
[6] ' Ann. Litt.'; also Connor, ' Letters.'

to thirteen or fourteen villages in the neighbourhood, where the clergy were roused to greater activity, and many conversions were made : they also sent missions into further Russia, but these had little success. The introduction of the Jesuits into Wilna by bishop Valerian had given the Society its first foothold in Lithuania; soon after Stephen's accession a second college was founded by Lithuania. Christopher Radziwill at Njeswicz on the Niemen, where the Jesuits attempted to remedy the deplorable system of early marriages. A third was established at Polock by the king, where they inaugurated a vigorous campaign against the Ruthenians, and induced many to forsake their 'popes.' From these colleges they made it a regular habit to visit villages in the neighbourhood on Sundays ; by this means they got at thousands who had never professed any religion before, except the relics of a primitive nature-worship. From Wilna they made frequent excursions into Samogitia, where the peasants were in a state of absolute ignorance. A fresh field of activity was opened up to them by Batory's conquest of Livonia and Esthonia ; he summoned the Jesuits to educate and convert his new subjects, Livonia. and powerfully aided them by the establishment of colleges at Riga and Dorpat, whence they had dreams of establishing a connection across Muscovy with the newly-formed missions of their brethren in India [1]. Here there was no lack of material to work upon, for the German population which had followed the trade enterprises of the Hanseatic League, and the conquests of the Teutonic Knights and Order of the Sword, was completely given over to Lutheranism. At Dorpat, Batory presented them with a church which had been intended by Ivan for the King of Denmark, and they were aided by Cardinal Radziwill and the Poles who accompanied Batory. Among Germans, Poles, Muscovites, and Esthonians they laboured with untiring zeal. The Lutherans had

[1] 'Annuae Litterae.'

declared it was impossible to learn the language of the last without the aid of magic ; the Jesuits set themselves to the task, and started a school to teach the language of the Letts, Russians, Swedes, and Lithuanians, besides Latin, German, and Polish [1].   Among the natives they met with considerable success ; traces of serpent-worship still survived, and it was customary to pray to the thunder and certain trees if there was a drought [2].   The Jesuits often won their way into the confidence of the rustics by their knowledge of medicine, which they utilised to effect many cures.   At Riga [3] they met with the bitterest opposition from the Lutherans, and the weapons which were so often afterwards employed against the Protestants were here turned against them ; their services were disturbed by unruly mobs ; more than once they were ejected from the city and their establishments pillaged.   The town authorities were no less hostile than the populace, but by degrees the Jesuits won over the council ; this did not mend matters much, for instead of being able to protect the Jesuits, the council itself was subjected to great annoyance.   On the death of Batory it was resolved to expel the Jesuits, giving them the choice between peaceable departure and forcible ejection.   The Society chose the former.   In spite of this reverse, the Jesuits had made enormous strides during this reign ; hitherto they had mainly confined themselves to the legitimate means of missionary propaganda ; Batory had been able to check attempts at persecution.   But in the next reign, secure of protection by those in authority whatever might happen, the Society began to exhibit more unlovely traits, and, like all sects which control political power, to use against its adversaries the methods not of persuasion but of persecution and proscription.

[1] 'Annuae Litterae.'   [2] Ibid.   [3] Ibid.; also Argentus.

CHAPTER V.

The King of the Jesuits.

THE election of Sigismund III to the throne proved to be
the greatest blow it was possible to inflict upon Protestanism
in Poland. Brought up by his mother, Catherine Sigismund III.
Jagiellon, in the strictest Roman Catholic doctrines, he made the promotion of the interests of Rome
the guiding motive of all his actions. This zeal for Rome
outweighed all considerations of prudence or policy; through
it 'he lost two hereditary thrones, and brought innumerable
calamities on the country which election had handed over
to him [1].' 'In order to make sure of heaven,' said the Emperor Ferdinand, 'he has renounced earth.' The Protestants
called him the 'king of the Jesuits,' and Sigismund gloried
in the appellation. This feeble imitation of Philip II of
Spain possessed all the bigotry and zeal of his model without
his abilities or strength of character. In all that he did
he was ruled by the Jesuits; he bestowed honours only on
those whom they favoured, and preferred their advice to
that of his wisest counsellors. 'By private interviews,' wrote
a Roman Catholic historian who was also bishop of Przemysl, 'which they could always command, the Jesuits so
bound the king by their solicitations, that he did everything
according to their counsel, and the hopes and cares of
courtiers had no weight except by their favour. They
moreover suggested what the king should determine in
public affairs with the greater peril to the state, because

---

[1] Salvandy, ' Histoire de Pologne avant et sous Jean Sobieski.'

persons were selected for the king's intimacy (especially his confessor and chaplain) from masters of religious novices, who were completely inexperienced in the position and affairs of Poland. This was alone the cause of errors not only in domestic but foreign policy, such as the king's relations with Muscovy, Sweden, and Livonia: yet it was considered almost sacrilege for anyone to blame their words or deeds, and no one who did not magnify them had easy access to office[1].' Chief among these advisers of the king

Peter Skarga.

was Peter Skarga[2], one of the most eminent of Polish Jesuits. Born in Masovia in 1536, he was educated at the University of Cracow, where he distinguished himself by winning the 'prima Laurea.' He then proceeded to Rome, where he entered the society in 1568. He began his preaching at Pultusk, and visited the colleges which Stephen had founded at Riga, Dorpat and Polock; his eloquence was very successful, and even now his sermons are thought highly of in Poland[3]. On the accession of Sigismund he became royal chaplain: he founded a confraternity of St. Lazarus at Warsaw, and many other establishments elsewhere. The union with the Greek Church now occupied his attention, and he used his position at the court[4] to convert many of those about the king. He subsequently resigned this position[5], and died September

The Nobles.

27, 1612, aged seventy-six years. His influence confirmed Sigismund in his resolution to grant no honours to any but zealous Roman Catholics, and this soon began to thin the ranks of the Protestant nobles: these converts often made up for lack of conviction by ostentatious zeal for their newly-adopted faith. Christopher Radziwill, who had been converted by Skarga, induced his younger brothers, George, afterwards cardinal and bishop

[1] Paulus Piasecius, ' Chronica Gestorum in Europa,' p. 299.
[2] ' Vita P. Skarga,' Cracow, 1661.　　　　[3] Morfill, ' Russia.'
[4] 'Vita P. Skarga,' p. 25.　　　　[5] Ibid. p. 29.

of Wilna and Cracow, Albert and Stanislas to abandon the
Helvetian Church; they signalised their conversion by a
holocaust of the heretical works their father had been
active in disseminating. Their example was followed by
other nobles, and as they had complete control over religion
on their estates, they frequently ejected all Protestants who
had settled there, and filled their places with Roman Catholics. This process was accelerated by the fact that the
Jesuits had got the education of the country entirely into
their hands, and great numbers of the nobles who were
now entering upon manhood had been educated in their
schools. With the aid of the nobles and government, the
Jesuits prosecuted their labours with unabated vigour and
increased success. By the year 1600 the numbers of the
Society had reached four hundred and sixty-six, and there
were establishments at seventeen different places, besides
the mission to the king's court and the staff of the Provincial, which were fixed in no one spot. In 1586 a
mission had been started at Dantzic, which, in Progress of the
spite of great opposition, was converted into Society.
a permanent college and made considerable progress,
especially through its missions in the neighbourhood.
Braunsberg had meanwhile become a centre of Jesuit
education; two schools had been established there, called
respectively the Pontifical and Warmiensian seminaries.
One of these was for the support of converted nobles who
were too poor to spend much on their own education, but
might be of great use to the Church[1]; they not only ap-
plied themselves to study, but also to more practical mani-
festations of their zeal, and on their return to their estates
turned out Protestant ministers and persuaded the people
to embrace Catholicism. The other seminary was chiefly
employed in educating youths from Sweden and Denmark[2],
who on their return took with them the seeds of the Roman

---

[1] 'Ann. Litt.' 1586, 1587. [2] 'Ann. Litt.' 1600.

D

Catholic religion. Both these schools were aided by the
canons of Warmia, who had welcomed the Society on its
first appearance in Poland. These establishments in Polish
Prussia were the occasion of continual disturbances. The
college at Dantzic was a constant bone of contention between the Jesuits and the town authorities [1]. The latter
maintained that this building, which had formerly belonged
to the Franciscans, was under their patronage, and that the
Jesuits had illegally gained possession of it [2]. The Society,
on the other hand, declared that this monastery was deserted
and half ruined when they entered it [3]; further, that they had
been established there by the king and bishop of Ladislav,
in contempt of whose authority the inhabitants had driven
them out. They were re-instated by the bishop, who was
also chancellor of the kingdom, but the townspeople again
drove them out and placed a guard over the building.
They had not recovered their foothold there by Sobieski's
reign [4], but a mission was in existence at Dantzic when the
Society was suppressed [5]. A no less bitter struggle was
waged at Thorn, where the bishop of Culm had established
the third Jesuit college in Polish Prussia. Riots broke
out, of which each side accused the other of being the
cause. Here also the Jesuits were expelled, but they regained their position, and were destined in after years to
cover themselves and the city with evil fame by an act of
horrible persecution. In Masovia the history of the Society
is much less eventful. A college had been founded at
Pultusk in the reign of Sigismund Augustus; to this was
added a college at Lomza on the Narew, and residences at
Warsaw, Rawa [6], and Krosna [7]. The Jesuits occupied them-

---

[1] Thuanus, part v, p. 1224.   [2] Cf. also Wengerscius.
[3] Argentus, chap. ix.   [4] Salvandy. 'Hist. de Pologne.'
[5] Guettée, vol. iii. Table at the end showing the numbers and
establishments of the Jesuits.
[6] On a tributary of the Bzura, S.W. of Warsaw, in the voivodie of
Rawa: later in Great Poland.   [7] Argentus, chap. viii.

selves with appeasing matrimonial quarrels, and teaching their pupils to perform tragedies before assemblies of nobles, which was found to be an excellent means of extracting voluntary gifts. A residence was established at Plock by its bishop[1], but none of these met with much opposition, and they were conspicuous neither through persecution of, nor by the Protestants. In Great Poland the school at Kalisz was in a flourishing condition ; in 1600 it contained five hundred pupils, with specially appointed professors to deal with Mathematics, Philosophy, Conscience-cases and Controversies[2] ; here, as elsewhere, they induced many boys to attend the school without the knowledge of their parents. At Posen the Society was employed in refuting the numerous writings which had appeared against them. Their history at Lublin and Cracow in Little Poland, at Lemberg and Iaroslav in Red Russia was very similar, and was marked by no very striking incidents, till at Cracow there broke out the famous quarrel between the Society and the University[3]. The union[4] with the Greek Church gave a powerful impulse to their labours in Lithuania. At Wilna, the school which in 1587 had seventy pupils, in 1600 counted over eight hundred, chiefly from the sons of the Lithuanian nobility, and was successfully competing with the Zwinglian establishment there. A mission was formed to Olita[5] and several places in Samogitia ; they had missions in forty-seven places in the neighbourhood, and according to their own account made more than seventeen hundred conversions in one year ; 'but,' complains Argentus, 'the people had a sad habit of frequenting the drink-shops on Sundays.' At Polock their number was increased by the flight of many from Livonia when the war with Sweden

---

[1] Argentus, p. 225. [2] 'Ann. Litt.' 1600.
[3] See Chapter VII, The Jesuits and Education.
[4] See Chapter VIII, The Jesuits and the Greek Church.
[5] On the Niemen, S.W. of Wilna.

broke out. A college had been founded at Orza[1] in White
Russia, but the proximity to Muscovy rendered the site
dangerous. There was a moveable residence at Smolensk
because of the wars, and the Society did good work among
the soldiers. They penetrated into the Ukraine, and
Stanislas Zolkiewski endeavoured to found a college at
Kiev, but the country was 'plena schismate, infecta haeresi,
polluta Judaismo[2],' and Roman Catholics were few and far
between. In Livonia there was a repetition of the scenes
enacted in Polish Prussia; a residence was formed at
Wenden[3], and in the country the Jesuits had it much their
own way, but in Riga and Dorpat even the powerful
patronage which they enjoyed was unable to save them
from persecution. Their expulsion from Riga on the death
of Batory led to endless litigation; in 1590 the disturbances
were temporarily allayed by a Royal commission, and the
Jesuits were recalled[4]; but this was by no means the end
of their troubles; the attempt to introduce the Gregorian
Calendar caused fresh tumults, and there was continual
friction[5] until Livonia passed under the sway of Sweden.
Their position was not improved by the war which broke
out with that power: most of them fled from Dorpat, but
the irritation caused by their proselytism and the policy
Sigismund had adopted, undoubtedly facilitated the transfer
of these provinces to the king of Sweden.

The preponderance which the Jesuits had now acquired
by their own efforts, the confidence of the king, and the
favour of the nobles, enabled them to have recourse to open

Persecution. persecution, which had been strongly condemned by the laws of the kingdom again
and again[6]. It is not easy to apportion the blame of these

---

[1] On the Dnieper, half way between Mohilew and Smolensk.

[2] Argentus, p. 29.　　　　[3] Venda in Latin, between Riga and Dorpat.

[4] Piasecius, pp. 52, 82.　　　　　　　　　[5] Argentus, chap. ix.

[6] 'Jura et Libertates Dissidentium in Religione in Regno Poloniae.'
1708. This little book gives a summary of these various enactments,.

proceedings with any degree of precision, and Protestant writers have been only too ready to attribute to the Society every occurrence which might bear the appearance of persecution ; nevertheless, to charge the Jesuits with gross persecution is not to accuse them of worse acts than were perpetrated in every country of Europe at that time. It is, however, by no means necessary to believe that the Jesuits directly instigated all the outrages that have been attributed to them. 'The people of Riga,' complained Argentus, ' hated Catholicism, and could not restrain themselves when they saw its rites performed.' This was no doubt true ; but the same might be said of Roman Catholic populations, and their hatred of the Protestants was not likely to be appeased by the fervid harangues in the streets which were among the favourite weapons of the Society. Hence it frequently happened that after one of these heated addresses, the mob signalised its zeal by making an immediate onslaught upon Protestant churches. It may sometimes have happened that these street preachers directly instigated these outrages[1], but more frequently the mob acted on its own impulse. Ascension Day[2] was the occasion of most of these outrages ; the Jesuits always celebrated that day with great pomp and ceremony. They organised huge processions, in which their pupils played a prominent part; images were carried out, and pictorial representations of scenes in ecclesiastical history or mythology ; pictures of the martyrdoms the Jesuits had endured ; illustrations of the life of Loyola and his reception into heaven. All these, united with special services and glowing harangues from the street orators, combined to rouse the

oaths, &c., securing liberty to all religions in Poland. 'Dissidentes' of course originally included Catholics: it was a mistake probably made on purpose, to limit it to non-Romanists.

[1] Wengerscius gives an instance, p. 223. 'In 1605 at Posen a Jesuit said, "The Magistrates will not, the Senate will not ; do you therefore, whoever you are in the crowd, reduce to smoke and ashes all the haunts of the heretics." ' [2] Ranke.

feeling of the mob to a fever heat, which after the ceremony found vent in a general attack upon the heretics. Their pupils naturally found in this a congenial occupation. At Cracow[1] the Reformed Church was attacked by them in 1574 and 1575, and again on Ascension Day 1587 and 1590. On the latter occasion many houses were burnt. The Protestants[2] sent delegates to the king, demanding that a place should be given them to worship in, and that a Diet should be summoned at which religious peace should be confirmed. Sigismund heard them with anger, and bitterly upbraided them for holding an assembly by their own authority, contrary to the laws of the kingdom. After this, the Protestants were compelled to take refuge in the neighbourhood; thither the students made frequent expeditions on Ascension Day, for the purpose of attacking and pillaging their churches. Sometimes they went out armed[3]; in 1611, they came into contact with the civil militia, and several were shot; on this occasion the riot lasted three days. Similar violence occurred in 1631 when Zamoyski pressed for a judicial investigation, but the influence of the Roman Catholic clergy prevented all enquiry. At Vilna an attempt at persecution was made, but Batory sent orders from Pskov that it should cease. Frequently funerals were attacked by the students, who dispersed the mourners, broke open the coffins, and treated the dead bodies in a dis-

Jesuit methods.

graceful manner[4]. Physical force was not, however, the only method resorted to by the Jesuits : they exhausted all the arts of sarcasm and ridicule to bring Protestant ministers into contempt. No sooner was a synod convened than letters appeared from the devil to the delegates; whenever a minister died, letters were published addressed from hell, and purporting to be written

[1] Wengerscius, pp. 232-236.   [2] Thuanus, part v, 135, 136.
[3] Wengerscius, p. 234.
[4] Wengerscius gives a long catalogue of outrages all over Poland, which it would be wearisome to recapitulate.

by him to the principal members of his congregation; in these writings the Jesuits adapted themselves to their public, and their coarse wit was often very effective.   Trained from their youth in dialectic and controversy, they were generally more than a match for their adversaries in the arts of public disputation; accordingly, they were always challenging the Protestants to such trials of skill and knowledge which usually redounded to their own advantage.   At last the Protestants grew more cautious, and avoided these encounters with their skilful and not over scrupulous opponents[1]. These measures were directed chiefly against ministers; laymen they sought rather to convert than to persecute, and often used gentler means.   They insinuated themselves into their confidence by their suave manners, their readiness to help in difficulties, often by their medical skill and the care they bestowed on the education of the children.   They were in the habit of making marriages between Roman Catholic ladies and Protestants, because, even if the husbands were not converted, the children were generally educated in the creed of their mothers.   No method, in short, was left untried which could bring back Protestants to the Church of Rome.

This success, and the means by which it was secured, did not contribute towards the internal peace of Poland : the Protestants were still numerous enough to form a powerful opposition, and they were joined by *The opposition.* a large number of Catholics who viewed with disgust the sway the Jesuits exercised over the king's mind, and the effect which their counsels produced upon the external and internal policy of the government.   This party was led by Zamoyski, 'who possessed great influence, as one who had never swerved from the religion of his ancestors, and to whom Sigismund owed his throne.   He was chancellor of the kingdom and, holding aloof from all factions, had

[1] Cf. 'De Lublinensi Disputatione,' 1624, Aug. 9, 10.

always guarded the liberties of the realm with the greatest faithfulness and consistency[1]'; but his influence with the king waned as that of the Jesuits waxed; it was, however, sufficient to prevent the open outbreak of hostilities during his lifetime. On his death Nicolas Zebrzdowski aimed at succeeding to his position and influence as leader of the opposition. In 1607 dissensions came to a head, and the opposition formed a Rokosz, a sort of armed confederation permitted by the constitution. They determined to elect a new king [2] unless Sigismund listened to their demands: they complained of the influence of the Jesuits, and of the violation of the rights and liberties of the Dissidents. 'The Complaints of Jesuits,' they said, 'were guided by foreign advice; they had disregarded municipal rights at Dantzic and Thorn; they were eager to create civil disturbances; they made alliances and marriages with the house of Austria to secure their own power; they relied on the Spanish Inquisition, and trusted more to human counsels than Divine Providence. These were the results of the Council of Trent, from which, as from Pandora's box, all manner of evils had spread over Europe: not that the decrees of that council were in themselves bad, but the method of their execution was, and this the Society claimed as its special function. So cunningly do they labour that their diligence and activity had become truly formidable to the Polish nobility, and all who adhere to their ancestral laws, and cleave to their primitive liberty. Hence arose the disturbances in the kingdom. The Society incited Batory to nefarious projects against his own people; it was the cause of conspiracies in every country in Europe, and it was to be feared that such would be the case in Poland. Zamoyski had done well to exclude them from the University he had founded, because he did not consider them fit to educate youths in the discipline of the country [3].'

(margin note: the Rokosz.)

---

[1] Thuanus, part v, 1223.   [2] Ibid. 1224.   [3] Ibid. 1299 et seq.

The Rokosz was not, however, agreed with respect to the Jesuits, and there were bitter altercations on the subject; finally it was decided that they should not be expelled from Poland, but be confined to the schools, that they might be free to devote themselves to education : one only was to be allowed at the king's court. In July, 1607, a battle was fought at Guzow, where Sigismund was victorious, and though Zebrzdowski kept the field for some time, he was powerless, and an amnesty was proclaimed. Piasecius [1] maintains that the object of the Rokosz was not principally against the decrees of the Council of Trent or the Jesuits, but to expel certain intimates of the king who introduced a foreign régime and punish the violation of certain laws. However this may be, its defeat gave the Catholic reaction a free hand, and henceforth to the death of Sigismund it pursued its course without let or hindrance ; henceforth the Protestants are a small and persecuted minority; they cease to be a considerable element in national life ; the policy of the country is entirely in the hands of the Jesuits : in other words, Poland ceases to have a national policy at all.

[1] 'Chronica Gestorum,' p. 247.

CHAPTER VI.

The Jesuits and their Critics in Poland.

THERE has probably never been an institution that has suffered more from extravagant praise and violent abuse than the Society of Jesus; and unfortunately this fate has pursued it to the present day : its apologists see no evil and its enemies see no health in it whatever. If an impartial attitude is rare now, the fact that men in the thick of the fight between Catholicism and Protestantism failed to appreciate their opponents and lavished upon them unstinted abuse, does not cause much surprise or call for loud denunciation. The Society by its constitution lent itself to extremes of praise and abuse; it consisted mainly of two very distinct classes of members, the 'professed,' who lived on alms and devoted themselves exclusively to spiritual labours, and the coadjutors, who stood lower in the hierarchy of the Order and managed its temporal affairs : these latter could acquire fixed revenues, and could mingle in secular matters of every description. It was their skill in temporal concerns which gave the enemies of the Society their principal weapons of attack, while the zeal and devotion of the 'professed' furnished its apologists with their strongest weapons of defence.

The success of the Jesuits in Poland was the signal for the outburst of a multitude of attacks which contain almost every charge that has been brought against the Society. There is one exception; those assertions of personal immorality which bulk so big in more recent denunciations of the Society are conspicuous by their absence. It is with different subjects that the Polish pamphleteers mainly deal. Many of these charges are similar to those brought against the Society in other countries, but some are peculiar to Poland. The Jesuits, declared a Catholic nuncio to the Diet in 1590 [1], made themselves arbiters of the election of the king, that they might afterwards employ the supreme authority for their own gratification; it was they who excited troubles at Riga, in Livonia, Lithuania, and Volhynia. At Cracow on the one hand they had made themselves masters of churches, turning out the priests who were in possession, without regard to age or infirmities; on the other hand it was at their instigation that the church granted by the king and Diet to the Lutherans had been set on fire. At Polock, in Lithuania, they robbed priests of their livings; in several parts of Little Russia they had seized on the most fertile lands and despoiled the richest citizens. They carried off from the houses of the nobles whatever was best and most precious. Their colleges were palaces and fortified citadels, as at Posen and Lublin, from which they seemed to threaten the neighbouring towns with war. Zamoyski had said that it was necessary to beware of admitting them to state affairs, while the bishop of Cracow thought the Society was trained to overthrow the doctrines of the Roman Catholic Church, excite seditions, oppress honest citizens, and vitiate good habits; their system of education was bad; obscure men were advanced to high positions, and their mediation had procured the peace with Muscovy.

[1] Crétineau-Joly declares that this was really a pamphlet by a Lutheran, and not a speech by a nuncio at all. This may be true; but the Society employed similar tactics, and published apologies purporting to be speeches of noble senators to the Diet. This seems to have been a favourite method of literary warfare; the defence of the Society was appropriately put in the mouth of a senator, as the Senate had become under Sigismund the centre of the Catholic reaction.

These charges elicited more than one answer [1] on behalf of the Society. A noble replied to the nuncio, and denied

Nobilis Poloni Oratio.

the genuineness of the opinions he had quoted against the Society. It never interfered in secular affairs except by the express command of the Pope, which it could not disobey. The Jesuits had stopped the spread of heresy in Poland, and had they arrived fifty years sooner, the country would have been saved countless troubles. Their system of education was approved of by the king and nobles of Poland, and was admirably adapted for its purpose. It was true that the Jesuits had negotiated the peace with Muscvoy, but no one found fault with it. They did indeed possess some country places which they looked after with great care, but there was no luxury of any description ; their fortified places were to secure them against the incursions of the Scythians. Stephen Batory did not raise the siege of Pskov because of tumults aroused by the Jesuits, but because negotiations for peace had been commenced. Most of these charges were derived from the benches of Dutch or English ships at Dantzic, Elbing, or Königsberg. Similarly false were the charges that the Jesuits favoured the Spanish monarchy, and put their devotion to it before their patriotism. Karnkowski, archbishop of Gnesen, Macieiowski, bishop of Luck, Christopher Radziwill, all showed their appreciation of the Society by founding colleges for its benefit. Nothing could be more false than that the Society was enormously rich ; all the liberality of the nobles only afforded its members a bare sustenance. As to their influence on the king's election, the Jesuits were present at Warsaw on private business, and took no part in politics ; it was the duty of Poles to extend to the Jesuits

---

[1] Stan. Roscius, 'Spongia qua absterguntur maledicta equitis Poloni contra Soc. Jes.' Also 'Nobilis Poloni pro Soc. Jesu clericis oratio prima.' Ingolstadt, 1590. The copy in the Bodleian is attributed to a 'Johannes Lans,' on what grounds is not stated, nor who Lans was. It probably emanated from a Jesuit, and was not a speech at all.

that liberty and protection which they gave to all religions, and to refuse to credit charges, maliciously and falsely brought against them.

These speeches or pamphlets are merely instances among a multitude, most of which have been lost, but there is an enquiry into the effects of the proceedings of the Society of Jesus in Poland, which, published towards the end of Sigismund's reign, is marked by considerable insight and great moderation[1]. The trouble in Poland, according to this author, was the same as elsewhere; all the disturbances of the last forty years had arisen from the decrees of *Consilium de recuperanda pace regni Poloniae.* the Council of Trent, or rather, from the method of their execution. The Tridentine reformation was opposed not only by religious feeling, but by various national privileges, liberties, laws, and customs. That the clergy of Poland were as zealous as any to carry out these decrees was shown by the synod of Piotrkow, 'quam seu Filiam Poloniae Medea illa Tridentina peperit'; and these decrees were a sign of what was coming. The kings of Poland joined the union of Catholic sovereigns, and made an especial alliance with Austria; hence arose internal dissensions in which the king was involved. But the Council of Trent and the alliance with Austria were in themselves no bad thing; it was the method of executing the Tridentine decrees that did the mischief, and for this the Jesuits were responsible. The form of the Society was monarchical; absolute obedience was required; the Jesuits recognised no superior but members of their own order, and these were generally Spaniards or Italians: they were 'ab utriusque Fori ordinaria jurisdic-

---

[1] 'Consilium de recuperanda et in posterum stabilienda pace regni Poloniae,' Mercure Jesuite, 1626. It was written about 1612 in Polish, and is based upon the demands of the Rokosz of 1607. It was afterwards translated into Latin, and appeared in the 'Mercure Jesuite.' Another translation, with additions, was made into Latin in 1632, and dedicated to Oxenstiern. Both these latter editions are in the Bodleian. The work is anonymous.

tione exempti,' and thus free from all legal control; only
adherents of Spain were elected to offices, and in subordinate
grades the people were promoted and not the nobles, because
their patriotism would be a hindrance to them. They
educated their converts to be little more than Spaniards or
Italians; and in France, for instance, they all sided with
the League. The Society was like a sword whose blade
was buried in Poland, while its hilt was wielded by the
hands of the Holy See and Spaniards, who could make
it obey their least nod; and it was intended to dominate
Europe, so that there should be never again any opportunity
of revolt from Rome. The obstacles to this project in
Poland were liberty and the laws by which it was maintained. Hence all the privileges of the Jesuits were granted
to enable them to overcome these obstacles. First they
establish themselves at court as confessor to the king or
queen, or at least tutor to the heir; or they attach themselves
to the most powerful persons in the kingdom. They took
care that their adversaries' complaints should either be
neglected or evaded. They build a number of churches,
schools, &c., in the chief towns, and see that their houses are
on the wall, in order to have access night and day, as is the
case at Cracow, Wilna, and Posen. They used the arts of
the demagogue and the confessional, and by these means
gained the strength of faction and favour of the curators who
presided over the Public Treasury, which gave them command of both private and public property. They did not
care for petty rewards, but secured many entire inheritances
as legacies. In Poland nothing was heard of their justifica-
tion of tyrannicide, because Sigismund was devoted to them;
but if he changed his mind, how long would he be secure?
Only so long as the Jesuits pleased. They were continually
setting the laws at naught when they stood in the way; their
conversion of heretics was due to gold and silver arguments,
plentifully supplied from Rome; their system of education

was ruinous ; many eminent Poles complained that they had to correct the faults of their Jesuit training by travelling. The only thing to be done was to expel them from Poland ; it was no good trying to bind them by laws : they obeyed none, not even their own, for instance the decree of the General Congregation of 1593 that 'Jesuits should abstain from temporal affairs.'

It was probably in answer to this attack that Argentus, who was visitor of the two provinces of Poland and Lithuania, wrote his book [1] on the state of the Society in Poland. It is the most important work on the subject, and is at once a description of the progress of the Society and a defence against its enemies. His object, he says, is to give an account of his visitation in Poland as he had done elsewhere, that the king may know the real state of the Society, that he might protect it with his royal authority, and that calumnies may be refuted ; the Society had been introduced by the wishes not only of the king but of the kingdom, and had been of great advantage to its best interests. Their enemies, however, not only abused them, but called into question the king's actions, and maintained the Jesuits to be dangerous to Poland. When first he came into the country and heard on every side accusations against the Society, he thought there must be some ground for them, but after diligent searching found none. The Society had two classes of enemies—the heretics, and Catholics who knew nothing about it ; and there were two classes of accusations brought against the Society in Poland—one common to all countries, the other peculiar to Poland. The chief of

Johannes Argentus.

[1] Johannes Argentus, 'Ad Sigismundum III Liber de statu Soc. Jesu in prov. Pol. et Lith.' This work first appeared in Poland at Cracow in the shape of a letter dated Feb. 14, 1615 : it was then expanded into this 'Liber,' published at Ingolstadt in 1616 ; both are in the Bodleian. From the title it is evident that the success of the Society in Poland had necessitated its division into two provinces.

them are that the Society mixes in politics ; that it presses its
counsels upon the king in secular matters ; it canvasses for
the promotion of its partisans to dignities ; it seeks favours
and accepts rewards ; it scatters evil doctrines, overflows
with riches, and is greedy for other people's goods ; it infringes
the privileges of the nobles, excites tumults, disturbs the
peace in many towns, and abets the dissolution of the
country. The first charge Argentus meets with a characteristic ' distinguo ' ; there are two kinds of politics, firstly,
that concerned with the very foundations of a State, which
are justice, prudence, and religion ; secondly, that which
concerns public administration. The Society did indeed
inculcate the first three, but no Jesuit ever mingled in the
second : it was forbidden by a decree of the General Congregation. But the Jesuits did exhort kings and princes to do
rightly, to have God ever before their eyes, to observe
justice and prudence, to be the champions of the oppressed,
guardians of minors and protectors of widows ; and whose
business was it to direct the king's conscience if not a
theologian's ? No member of the Society ever advised the
king on purely political matters. Two years before, at the
Diet of Warsaw, Sigismund was asked whether it were true
that the Jesuits gave him counsel, and if so, he was requested
for the future not to listen to them, and thus crown his acts
of kindness to the Society. The king replied 'that it was
false to say that the Society interfered in politics or can-
vassed for the promotion of this or that individual ; if they
did, it would avail nothing, for he had his own methods and
reasons of promotion ; those rumours arose only from sus-
picions and false conjectures, and were of no weight.' As
to this latter accusation, the defence of Argentus is the
' reductio ad absurdum ' of refinement ; the Jesuits, he says,
never concerned themselves about preferments ; but they
sometimes addressed a humble question as to whether the
person to be promoted was worthy of preferment, or ven-

tured to remind the king of good service done, in order that no one might be deprived of due reward from lack of access to the king; but these favours they only conceded to importunity, and if their partisans were promoted, it was through their own merits, not the intervention of the Society. Far from its being dangerous to States, the removal of the Society was always followed, as in Portugal and Transylvania, by national calamities; it was they who gave godly counsels to princes, and were, so to speak, their guardian angels. No less erroneous was the idea that the Jesuits were rich[1]; there were in Poland abbeys and monasteries whose revenues equalled that of a whole Jesuit province; there was not a college which, deducting necessary expenses, could maintain sixty people, allowing sixty florins a year to each. These colleges were burdened with debt, and for that reason freqûently could not be completed. In all Poland they have scarcely a house fit to live in, and their college at Posen, which was the chief one in Poland, was so badly off for buildings that of its sixty members more than half live in huts more suited for mice than men; at Wilna, where their college was burnt down, they had nothing to shelter them from the snows. Complaints had been made in the local assemblies, as in the Diet, that they excited disturbances and were ruining the kingdom. These tumults were not, however, to be laid at their door; at Dantzic it was the populace who set at naught the king's authority; at Thorn, it was again the citizens who attacked the Jesuits, not the Jesuits the citizens. At Riga, the Jesuits made an attempt to come to an agreement about their church, but the town authorities kept procrastinating, and no conclusion was arrived at. It was prejudice that caused so many libels against the Society, and led some nobles to complain of the infringement of their liberties and 'praejudicium omne judicium tollit.' The Jesuits did

---

[1] Krasinski says they could reckon £100,000 of yearly income.

E

excellent work by their missions ; in Livonia they were the only Christian ministers in many places; the country was vast and there was no one to take care of souls ; in White Russia there were many Catholics of great age who had never taken the communion, because their lords did not consider it a food for peasants.

This was indeed the strong point in the defence of the Society ; it paid more heed to the peasant than did the Protestants, and its missions were unrivalled. But to attain to an end which the Jesuits considered good, they were not scrupulous as to means, believing that the former justified the latter ; in spite of denials, it is fairly certain that the Society did take an active part in politics ; it was admitted that they could do so by the command of the Pope, and this interference in politics was almost wholly mischievous.

CHAPTER VII.

The Jesuits and Education in Poland.

Of the three main objects which Loyola set before the Society of Jesus, preaching, confessing, and education, the last was the most important. Preaching and the confessional were already among the favourite weapons of the Roman Catholic Church, but the Jesuits were to make of education an instrument more potent than any other in the conversion of heretic and schismatic. It was this educational object that rendered necessary the establishment of the spiritual coadjutors who, unlike the professed members, could live in fixed residences, acquire revenues, and were not bound by the obligation to devote themselves to continual travelling in the service of the Pope; they could establish themselves in any place, become residents, gain influence, and put themselves at the head of instruction[1]. This was one of the most important institutions of the Society, and contributed more than any other to its success. In Poland the main object was the education of young nobles. Wherever they went, their first and greatest anxiety was to get hold of the education of the young, because this secured their ultimate if not immediate success; but in Poland there was an additional reason for zeal in getting into their hands the instruction of young nobles. Here every pupil was a potential petty despot; the nobility had absolute control over religion on their

Importance of Education.

---

[1] Ranke, vol. i. 149, 150.

estates, and the prevailing faith was not necessarily that of the government but that of the majority of nobles; every pupil secured by the Jesuits meant at some time or other an estate with all its inhabitants brought over to Rome. Hence, no sooner was the Society established in Poland than schools for the nobility began to rise in every quarter.

Jesuit Schools. At Pultusk there was a school which contained four hundred pupils all noble [1]. At Wilna, in 1600, the Jesuits had eight hundred scholars [2], chiefly sons of the Lithuanian nobility, many of whom were heretics; in the school at Kalisz [3] there were five hundred pupils. At Posen they were welcomed by a heretic noble, who told them that there had been a Lutheran school there for twenty-six years which had done no good in the town [4]. Seminaries had also been established at Braunsberg, Dorpat, and Polock [5], and many other places for the same object. The education the Jesuits gave was gratuitous; but they received large gifts from nobles, especially on occasions when their pupils gave public performances of tragedies and recitations before assemblies of the nobility [6]; and these gifts gave their enemies occasion to say that while they reaped all the credit of gratuitous education, the presents they received brought them more than any tariff of fees could have done. This liberality brought them many partisans even among Protestants and members of the Greek Church, who were induced to send their children to the Jesuit schools by the fact that many had completed their studies there without abandoning their creed. The Society not only received them, but endeavoured to attract Protestant children by all means in its power; at several places they were induced to attend without the knowledge of their parents. The Jesuits treated them with great courtesy and kindness, and kept them as long as possible

---

[1] 'Annuae Litterae'; also Ranke.   [2] 'Ann. Litt.'   [3] Ibid.
[4] Ibid.   [5] Ibid.   [6] Ibid. passim.

under their control; wherever they came across a boy of
promise they endeavoured to secure him for the Society.
At Wilna a young noble in a riot proclaimed himself a
Protestant and ready to die for his religion; the Jesuits
preserved him from harm, treated him kindly, and finally
succeeded in converting him, so that he became one of
their most distinguished members. In this way the Society
soon outstripped all the other schools in the country, and
began to aim at getting the Universities into its hands.
This was the cause of considerable friction with   Quarrel
the University authorities, especially at Cracow,   with the
where open fights took place more than once   Universities.
between Jesuit scholars and members of the University.
These physical contests led to a literary warfare, in which
the Society and the University charged each other with
being the cause of disturbances; students from the latter,
maintained the Society, attacked the college and did great
violence, tearing down the theses of St. Thomas Aquinas,
and committing other outrages[1]. These charges were
answered by a manifesto on behalf of the University of
Cracow, which summarises the accusations made against
the Jesuit methods of education, and it at least is not open
to the imputation of having been written by Lutherans and
ascribed to Catholics. The professions of charity towards
the University, maintains the author, are a mockery, for
charity is departed since the Jesuits came. They have
filled the land with their schools, and, not satisfied with
this, they libel a college which does not belong to them[2].
Because Cracow was the chief town in Poland, they thought
it necessary that it should become the centre of Jesuit education. The Academy had refused to participate in the
ceremonies of the canonisation of St. Ignatius, because it

[1] 'Manifestatio contra Univ. Crac.' 1622. Mercure Jesuite, 1626–1630.
Geneva.
[2] 'Responsio ad libellum Jesuitae.' Mercure Jesuite: also a separate
edition.

was a snare of the Jesuits. They aimed at getting all the
education of the country in their power, and had already declared that they had possession of the University of Cracow,
and their insolence warned its members to beware of their
endeavours. Cracow had produced greater men than all the
Jesuit colleges put together : such were Hosen, Cromer the
historian, Orzechowski, and others ; it had given the Society
its Skargas, Herbestos, and Laternas, men whom the present
degenerate schools of the Jesuits could never produce. It
had a clean record for more than two hundred years, while
the Jesuits had already produced a disastrous effect upon the
University of Paris. There was all the difference in the world
between the nature of the Society of Jesus and that of the
University : ' Academiae omnia aperta, candida, simplicia :
illis clausa, cauta, tecta.' The Jesuits sought the courts of
princes, students sought solitude; fire and water would
agree better than the Society and the University. The
Jesuits had persecuted the heretics, and when they were
lacking, turned to the Academy ; if a man looked askance
at a Jesuit they wished to excommunicate him ; if he protested against the Fathers he was declared to have violated
ecclesiastical liberties. They spread false reports over
Poland, and taught women in their apartments, the mob
in the gutters, and boys at school, that no one could be
saved unless he favoured the Jesuits. They made Loyola
the equal of the Apostles, and deprived Christ of his glory,
with the same zeal as they robbed the University of its
rights. They sought honours of all kinds and riches from
the king. They had ruined all true learning in Poland,
' desiere literae, desiit eruditio'; their learning was only fit
for women and boys, ' species virtutis pro re est, fucus pro
veritate ' ; they taught their pupils miserable tragedies,
declamations and rhymes, and exhibited weak plays on the
stage. They had robbed parents of their children and the
University of its sons, and made them such that no one

regretted their loss ; men who would have become great senators had they remained at the University, were enticed away and turned into mediocre Jesuits. They had ruined the school at Posen, and caused riots at Lublin and Wilna, the least of which they exaggerated to excite odium against their enemies. They were supple courtiers, and by the favour they curried with the great and their denunciations in every church and school they possessed in the land, sought to ruin the University of Cracow.

On this occasion, however, the Jesuits met with a rebuff, for at the Diet of Warsaw [1], on March 4, 1626, the question was raised and considerable hostility evinced towards the Society by the nuncios. One declared that there were already more Jesuit colleges than he liked ; the Palatine of Cracow said there was one Palatine, one Academy, one Rector, and about the Jesuit school he wished to know nothing ; another deputy expressed his opinion that as a devout Roman Catholic he considered these commotions had nothing to do with the Pope, who did not wish to interfere ; it was the interest of the Republic to calm tumults, secure peace to the royal city, shut up the Jesuit school, and support the University. Another declared that the Jesuit schools should be shut up not only at Cracow but throughout the whole of Poland. Finally, it was decreed that the Jesuits should shut up their school at Cracow, and cease from molesting the University. The Society immediately sent delegates to ask the Pope to absolve them from obedience to this decree, as it would be their certain ruin. All the states of the realm and nuncios of the provinces protested that their privileges were being invaded, and that an attempt was being made to ruin the University of Cracow by means of a Jesuit school. In 1627 [2] the University wrote to that of Louvain that they

Decree against the Jesuits.

[1] 'Mercure Jesuite,' 1626, 1630. Geneva.
[2] Ibid. 1630. Geneva.

were in the same danger; for seven years the Jesuits had
been attacking the University of Cracow; they had recourse
to force and the arts of the courtier when deceit did not
succeed; they persuaded the king that the University was
the greatest enemy of the Society and even of His Majesty
himself; everywhere the same representations were made.
The Society had two things in its favour, the goodwill of
Sigismund and of Rome. More than once they had deluged
the city with innocent blood, and soon all true learning would
be abolished and all knowledge lost. This was but an
episode in the struggle which went on all over Europe
between the Jesuits and the Universities; but the resistance of Cracow came too late; it had looked on heedless
while the Society crushed all other elements of opposition,
and now it had to stand alone, with the natural result that
the Jesuits were in the end successful, and education in
Poland passed entirely into their hands until the revival in
the eighteenth century.

It is a commonly received opinion that the devotion of
the Society to education was a partial set-off against its mischievous influence on politics and morals; there
is considerable authority to support this view.
Bacon declared that 'in that which regards the
education of youth it would be more simple to say "consult
the schools of the Jesuits, for there can be nothing better
than is practised there,"' and Leibnitz expressed a somewhat similar opinion. There can indeed be no doubt that
the Jesuits were by far the most effective educationalists
during the sixteenth and seventeenth centuries; their
methods were more organised, and they paid more heed
to education than any other body of men; but it may be
questioned whether its merits counterbalanced its defects.
It was if anything too rigidly systematic, and tended to
reduce or to raise all men to the same level; this was of
course the chief aim of the Society, and its methods gave

Effects on Education in Poland.

a marked and uniform impress to all who fell under its
influence. If this was calculated to benefit men of ordinary
abilities, it exerted a very depressing influence upon men
of talent and genius. Hence it followed that of all the able
men who entered the Society very few became great men
of letters[1]. This was conspicuously the case in Poland; it
did indeed produce two men of note, Sarbiewski, born in
1595, who is considered the best of modern Latin poets,
and was employed by Urban VIII to correct hymns for a
new breviary, subsequently becoming professor at Wilna,
and Smiglecki, who wrote on logic; but this is a poor
record, considering the Society had complete control of
education in Poland for more than a century and a half.
By the end of Sigismund's reign literature had declined as
rapidly as it had risen during the reign of Sigismund
Augustus. It was the education of the Jesuits which
made Latin the prevalent language among the Polish
nobles[2], and a real national literature is next to impossible
when the habitual language of the educated part of the
population is a foreign one. This use of Latin introduced
a barbarous admixture of words, and created a no less
barbarous style called the Macaronic. Polemical divinity
occupied the attention of the pupils of the Jesuits, and
instead of acquiring useful knowledge they wasted their
time in dialectic subtleties and quibbles, while the flattery
lavished on their benefactors and abuse bestowed on their
enemies, rendered their style bombastic in the last degree.
The classical productions of the sixteenth century were not
reprinted for more than a century, during which period
there was no national literature. This system of education
failed to produce any enlightened statesmen, and it failed

---

[1] Mariana on the defects in the government of the Society of Jesus.
There is both a French and Spanish version in the 'Mercure Jesuite,'
1630.
[2] Connor, 'Letters on Poland.' He also illustrates the ignorance of
the Poles on medicine, philosophy, &c.

to overcome the invincible ignorance and blind prejudices of the ruling caste. It was a period marked by no efforts at reform ; on the contrary, sound notions of law and right became obscured, and gave way to absurd ideas of privilege, by which liberty degenerated into licence, while the peasants sank into a state of predial servitude. The virtue and science to which, according to Crétineau-Joly[1], the Jesuits train d these Frenchmen of the North, are at the same time a striking illustration and condemnation of the merits of the system of education pursued by the Jesuits.

[1] Crétineau-Joly, vol. iv. p. 132.

CHAPTER VIII.

THE JESUITS AND THE GREEK CHURCH.

DURING the long anarchy which preceded the fall of Poland, it became a common saying that 'Poland maintained itself on its disorder.' It may be said with greater truth that Poland during the golden age of Sigismund Augustus and Batory maintained itself by its toleration. Consisting mainly as it did of the adherents of two antagonistic Churches, toleration was for Poland a 'sine qua non' of its existence. For the partisans of one to have recourse to persecution and proscription against the adherents of the other, was to introduce an element which could not fail to act as a powerful solvent upon a state like Poland. This is precisely what happened. All idea of toleration was swept away by the wave of Catholic reaction : when missionary propaganda failed to convert and temporal rewards to seduce the members of the Greek Church, their treatment by the dominant sect became such that they viewed not merely with indifference but with glad acquiescence their subjection to a foreign power. Persecution overcame the cohesion which bound them to Poland, and set free the centrifugal forces which were always its weakness, and now became a potent cause of its ruin.

The union of the Greek and Latin Churches had always been one of the cherished aims of successive Popes, but it

Need of toleration.

was an object that had never yet been accomplished. The union which Isidor had negotiated at the Council of Florence had never been more than a phantom, and its adherents even in Lithuania were inconsiderable. The outbreak of the Reformation and its rapid spread turned for a while the attention of Rome elsewhere, and absorbed all its energies; but the success of the Jesuits, especially in Poland, again brought the union within the range of practical politics. Several attempts had meanwhile been made to effect an understanding between the Greek and Protestant Churches, but they had all proved futile[1]. In their dealings with the Greek Church, the Jesuits made the union of 1439 their basis of operations. They carried on their work in a slightly different manner from that Methods of which they employed with the Protestants. the Jesuits. The same influences were brought to bear upon the nobles, the hope of temporal rewards and the education of their children. Possevino had founded in Lithuania a special seminary for Muscovites and several others, and these schools furnished valiant champions for the union[2]. But the Greek bishops were treated very differently from the Protestant ministers. At first the Jesuits did not attempt to convert, but merely to win them over to their view regarding the union, which was their immediate object; they thought that union would lead to unity, and unity to uniformity. The arts of seduction were employed instead of those of persecution. They were promised seats in the Senate beside the Roman Catholic bishops; their liturgy and special usages were to be preserved for them, on condition of their submission to the Holy See; and these prospects, united with the idea of freedom from disturbance, sufficed to win over several bishops and nobles.

[1] Wengerscius, p. 479. Thuanus. Letters between them were discovered by the Roman Catholics.
[2] 'Vicissitudes de l'Église Cath. en Pologne,' with preface by Montalembert; also 'Vie du Père Possevin.' Paris, 1712.

At this time the two chief prelates of this Church were Onesiphorus, metropolitan of Kiev, and Cyril Terlecki, bishop of Luck [1], both of whom were married. The Patriarch Jeremiah on his return from Moscow deposed Onesiphorus, and consecrated in his stead Michael Ragoza [2], who was presented to him by the Lithuanian nobles. Terlecki succeeded in concealing his marriage and maintaining himself in his bishopric. Ragoza seems to have been an honest but weak and vacillating man, peculiarly liable to be influenced by the arguments which the Jesuits, and especially Skarga, brought to bear on him. He was further unsettled by the appointment of Terlecki as Exarch, which diminished his own authority. The bishop of Luck was not more satisfied with his position : on the one hand he was engaged in a quarrel with Ostrogski, the pillar of Greek orthodoxy ; on the other he was subject to persecution from the bailiff of Luck, who had been converted to Romanism ; at the same time he dreaded the exposure of the deception he had employed with the Patriarch in order to escape deposition [3] at a council which the latter had summoned. Under these circumstances he and several other bishops determined to take a step which would at least secure them the peaceful possession of their sees, and de- The Union of Brześć. clare for the union. They laid their project before Ragoza, but the metropolitan with characteristic indecision kept up negotiations with both parties ; an attack by Ostrogski drove him into the arms of Terlecki, who with Potiei his zealous abettor in the enterprise proceeded to Rome, where

[1] Lutsk, or Luceoria in Latin.

[2] Krasinski says he was a pupil of the Jesuits, who entered the Greek Church, and was rapidly promoted by their influence, in order that he might bring about the union; he quotes a long letter to him from the Jesuits of Wilna, but this only proves what is admitted, that Ragoza kept up negotiations with both parties. The above account follows Rambaud, Karamsin, vol. x. 380, and Mouravieff, 'Hist. of the Russian Church,' p. 138 sqq.; these say Ragoza was presented for election by the Lithuanian nobility; Krasinski that Sigismund unconstitutionally appointed him.   [3] Mouravieff.

they were received with great pomp by Clement VIII. The
Opposition of union was not however accomplished without
the Greek great opposition. 'The success of the Jesuits
Church. had stimulated the adherents of the Greek
Church to strenuous measures of self-defence. Religious
confraternities were formed which took an energetic part
in the struggle with the Jesuits; they had their elected
chiefs, their common treasury, and they began to found
schools, to establish printing-presses, and to disseminate
polemical and pious works. They entered into friendly relations and formed ties with the Patriarchs of the East; they
used the power of a democracy in opposition to the
bishops appointed by the king, keeping a strict watch upon
and reprimanding them, and denouncing to orthodox Chris-
tendom the carelessness of their manners and religion. The
most celebrated of these confraternities were those of
Lemberg in Galicia, of Wilna in Lithuania, and Luck in
Volhynia. The one at Kiev founded there the great ecclesiastical academy of Little Russia[1].' Prince Ostrogski headed
this opposition to the union. Rival synods were held at
Brześć at different times; the orthodox excommunicated
the uniates, while the uniates replied by anathematising
the orthodox. From this time a bitter struggle began between the two parties: the Eastern Church opposed schools
of its own to the schools of the Jesuits, propaganda to propaganda; it preached and it printed. The uniate Rucki
was replaced even at Kiev by Peter Mohila, who had been
an old soldier, and knew how to repress by force contempt
of his authority. In 1633 he made into a college like
those of the Jesuits the school which had been founded
by the confraternity at Kiev, instituted professors of Greek,
Latin, and Philosophy, and made it the intellectual centre
of Western Russia. The consecration of Mohila as metropolitan by Jeremiah completed the separate organisation of

[1] Rambaud.

the two branches of the Greek Church in Poland. The rights and privileges of the Eastern branch were solemnly confirmed by the Diets of 1607 and 1608 ; the king was bound not to grant any dignities or offices in the Russian provinces of the Church, except to inhabitants professing its tenets ; its possessions were declared inviolable, and a tribunal composed of the adherents of both Churches was appointed to repress acts of hostility between the respective religions. These decrees were, however, openly set at defiance ; the king himself connived at contempt of his own and the Diet's authority when that offence was committed by the Jesuits and their partisans, and was often powerless to punish similar disregard on the part of their opponents. At Mohilew the clergy who acknowledged the union were expelled, and the names of the Pope and King in the Liturgy were replaced by those of the Patriarch and Sultan of Turkey. At Vitebsk the bishop Koncewicz was murdered in the streets on July 12, 1623. These outrages were equalled by those committed by Roman Catholic mobs, whose zeal was stimulated by the daily preaching of the Jesuits. They were powerfully aided by Rucki, who had been converted and became uniate metropolitan of Kiev, and Koncewicz, whose persecutions provoked a riot in which he lost his life. The extravagances of the latter prelate called forth a letter from Prince Leo Sapicha, who had been converted from Protestantism. His benefactions to the Society of Jesus are celebrated by Argentus and others, so that his testimony is not vitiated by undue partiality for the heretics and schismatics. He condemns the bishop's violence and disobedience to the laws   Effects of of Poland, and charges him with despoiling the   the Union. heretics, cutting off their heads, shutting up churches, abusing the authority of the king, and then appealing to the secular arm when his proceedings caused tumults. This union,' he wrote, ' has created great mischief . . . You have alienated the hitherto loyal Cossacks, you have brought danger on the country and perhaps destruction on the Catholics. The union has produced not joy but only discord, quarrels, and disturbances : it would have been better had it never taken place . . . It has already deprived us of Starodub, Severia, and many other towns and fortresses. Let us beware that this union do not cause your and our destruction [1].' The union of Brześć was indeed a disintegrating force in Lithuania; the approximation of the Lithuanian nobles to the aristocracy of Poland in character and institutions which preceded and accompanied the union of Lublin, like the thin edge of the wedge, began to separate them in feeling from the mass of the population ; and this wedge was driven in further by the union of Brześć, their desertion of the orthodox Church, and the persecution which followed in the wake of the Jesuits. Hitherto the Greek Church had furnished Poland with some of its most valiant defenders [2], not only against the Turk but against the Muscovite. 'When your Majesty,' said a nuncio at the Diet of Warsaw in 1620, ' makes war upon the Turk, from whom do you obtain the greater part of your troops ? From the Russian nation which holds the orthodox faith, from that nation which, if it does not receive relief from its sufferings and an answer to its prayers, can no longer continue to make itself a rampart for your kingdom. How can you beg it to sacrifice all to secure for the country the blessings of peace, when in its homes there is no peace ? Everyone sees clearly the persecutions that the old Russian nation suffers for its religion ; in large towns our churches are sealed up and the church domains are pillaged ; from the monasteries the monks have departed, and cattle in their stead are quartered within them. . . For twenty years in each dietine, in each Diet we have asked for our rights and

[1] Krasinski, 'Ref. in Poland,' ii. 192, 193.
[2] Lelewel, 'Hist. de la Lithuanie.'

liberties with bitter tears, and for twenty years we have not
been able to obtain them[1].' In addition to persecution
by the Roman Catholic missionary, the serfs were subject
to the scourge of the Jew, whom the noble made steward
of his lands, and to whom he had given the right of life and
death over his subjects. Robbed by the Jew, persecuted
by the Jesuit, and enslaved by the noble, the peasants
flocked in crowds to the Cossacks of the Ukraine.

These Cossacks had received a regular organisation under
Stephen Batory, but the proselytising zeal of the Jesuits
and the encroachments of the nobles did not   Revolt
leave them long in peace, and zealous in the   of the
cause of the Greek Church, they began to look   Cossacks.
to the Tsar of Moscow as an ally if not as a sovereign.
They found a leader in Bogdan Chmielnicki, who had been
able to obtain no redress for the wrongs inflicted upon him
by one of the nobles. The government had, indeed, wished
to come to terms with the Cossacks, but was unable to
restrain the nobles and the Jesuits. Ladislas himself was
powerless to help them, and advised Bogdan to seek redress
by his sword. His influence deferred the outbreak till after
his death; but during the reign of Casimir the Poles were
again and again defeated, the population of the Ukraine
flamed out in fierce revolt, while the orthodox clergy
preached a crusade against Jews and uniates. The war
dragged on with varied success but unvaried horror. The
Cossacks, unable to maintain themselves against Poland,
sought the protection and suzerainty of the Tsar Alexis, and
in 1667, by the treaty of Andruszowo, Russia gained possession of Smolensk and Kiev on the right bank of the
Dnieper, and all the Little Russian left bank. ' Thus,'
says Karamsin, ' Clement VIII, Sigismund, and Possevino,
working with zeal on behalf of the Western Church, con-

---

[1] Rambaud, ' Hist. of Russia,' vol. i. 366.

tributed involuntarily to the aggrandisement of Russia [1].'
The revolt of the Cossacks was the first indication of that
dissolution of Poland which was the result of the Catholic
reaction and policy of the Jesuits; it is the first indication
that the growth of Poland towards the East has ceased,
and the growth of Russia towards the West has begun.
Muscovite autocracy was distasteful to the Cossacks, but it
was better than oppression by noble and persecution by
priest, which was their lot under the sway of Poland.

[1] Karamsin, vol. x. 387 (French translation).

CHAPTER IX.

The Jesuits and the Constitution.

It has been remarked by one [1] of the historians of the Jesuits, that it is only under a strong government, whether a monarchy or republic, that the Society of Jesus is seen to perfection; for then, free from disturbance on the part of their enemies, the Jesuits devote themselves exclusively to apostolic labours. In other words, the Society prefers to be supported by a strong government if possible. This is natural, but it is none the less true that the Jesuits won their most striking success in a country which was 'an elective kingdom governed by anarchy,' where there was scope for other than purely apostolic labours. They arrived in Poland at a crisis not only of its religious but of its constitutional history. The line of the Jagiellons was on the eve of extinction, and the monarchy was about to lose the little power it possessed. The attempt which Casimir IV had made to free the royal authority from oligarchic tutelage by summoning the lesser nobles to a share in political power, was fraught with disastrous consequences [2]. The extinction of the Jagiellonian line and decrease of monarchical power, which had relied on the dietines as a counterbalance to the Diet, was not followed by the increase in power of the latter over the former. One

State of the Constitution.

---

[1] Crétineau-Joly. [2] Karéiev, 'Revue Historique,' 1891.

class only was represented in these bodies, and this enabled the nobles to employ the authority of the State as the instrument of their caste interests, to the exclusion of those of all other classes, and prejudice of those of the country. A single class had monopolised all political power, but it did not know how to organise itself[1]. Instead of strengthening the Diet in 1573, the nobles hastened to divide its power equally among all the gentlemen of the land. It was deprived of the right of interfering in the relations between nobles and peasants ; the former were granted supreme control over their subjects ; they could establish what religion they pleased upon their estates, and each became a petty despot, independent and absolute ; at the same time the principle, ' neminem captivabimus nisi jure victum,' the boasted palladium of Polish liberty, practically secured them from judicial prosecution[2]. The dietines had no power over individual nobles, and the Diet had none over the dietines. It assumed the form of an international congress of ambassadors, delegated by countries entirely autonomous[3]. The dietines began to give their nuncios ' mandats impératifs ' to oppose all measures distasteful to the constituencies, and the development of the 'liberum veto'[4] enabled each dietine to stop all national business until its claims had been satisfied, and when several nuncios refused to assent to the transaction of any business till the claims of the constituency of each had been settled, the deadlock became complete, and the Diet frequently separated without having come to a single resolution. The Diet apparently sovereign was practically impotent. ' Nothing rules it,' wrote Rousseau a century later, ' but nothing obeys it.' Laws innumerable were passed securing religious liberty to all creeds ; occasionally they were obeyed ; generally they

[1] Karéiev, ' Revue Historique,' 1891.   [2] Connor, 'Letters on Poland.'
[3] Karéiev, ' Revue Historique,' 1891.   [4] Ibid.

were disregarded. Catholic mobs pillaged Protestant churches; Protestant mobs drove the Jesuits from their cities and rifled their colleges. Sometimes these outrages were punished; more frequently they were not. Under a system like this ordinary methods were inadequate; but the Jesuits were equal to the task; with their habitual insight they perceived the salient points of the situation, and skilfully adapted their means to the end. The first requisite was to get control over the king. The King.

The intrigues of Commendoni [1], and the success with which he played upon the mutual jealousies of the Protestants, prevented the election of one of their number as king after the death of Sigismund Augustus. The effect of Batory's election was at once neutralised by the promptness with which he was converted to Catholicism. But their efforts were not attended with complete success till the election of Sigismund III [2]. To secure a king who gloried in the appellation of King of the Jesuits was not to win the battle; Poland was not to be converted merely by the conversion of the government, as was the case in some countries; but it was to secure the principal coign of vantage on the field of battle. Of the powers which were still left to the king, the distribution of the starosties, the 'panis bene merentium,' was the most important. It had been repeatedly urged on Batory that he should bestow places in the Senate exclusively on Roman Catholics [3], but that king, either from disinclination or consciousness of lack of power to carry out so extreme a policy, had consistently refused. Sigismund III had no such scruples, and control over these honours became a most powerful weapon in the hands of the Jesuits. The Senate became the centre of reaction, and through it Sigismund sought to govern. The The Senate. bishops, who were appointed by the king, were always chosen from among the most zealous partisans of the Jesuits. The

[1] K asinski.   [2] Ranke.   [3] Ibid. ii. 255, 256.

same principle was followed with regard to secular preferment ; Protestants were rigidly excluded, and the greater a
noble's zeal on behalf of the Jesuits, the greater his chance
of temporal rewards. Many families rose to power in this
way through their munificence towards the Society of Jesus.
Such were the Kostkas, Dzialinskis, and Konopats[1], and these
exercised a powerful influence upon others. It was chiefly
by skilful use of the royal power that the Jesuits sought to
secure the nobles, and through them the religion of Poland ;
but the struggle had to be fought out not merely at the
Court and in the Diet, but in every voivodie of the kingdom,
and here the early hold which they had acquired over education served them in good stead, for most of the nobles now
entering upon manhood had been educated in their schools,
and were devoted to their interests ; and thus they were
strong enough to maintain themselves in spite of the constant complaints which were being brought against them in
the dietines no less than in the Diet[2]. The struggle in the
towns was of longer duration ; here they had
none of the advantages which they possessed

The Towns.

in the country. The most influential people were not
nobles who had been educated in their schools ; and, living
under separate institutions, and being in large part German,
the principal inhabitants were not so open to the mercenary
arguments which Sigismund found very effective with the
nobles ; nevertheless ' in the royal towns,' says a Papal instruction, ' the inhabitants were compelled to change their
religion, though not by open violence[3].' Besides the royal
power and the Senate there was a third institution which
became a powerful support to the order—the judicial tribunals. It was comparatively easy for the
Jesuits after the accession of Sigismund to

Justice.

procure the election—for they were elective—of zealous

---

[1] Ranke, ii. 259.   [2] Argentus. ' De Rebus Soc. Jesu,' chap. ix.
[3] Ranke, ii. 276.

Roman Catholics to fill these tribunals, and this was an important gain because of the continual litigation which was going on between the Protestants and Roman Catholics. The churches were the chief subjects of dispute[1]; the Catholics claimed as their own all the churches that had once belonged to the Roman Church, and this claim the Protestants naturally resisted, and case after case was brought before the courts. As might have been expected from their composition, the verdict was generally in favour of the Catholics, and by degrees the Protestants were deprived of most of their churches in the country, and were frequently driven to worship in private rooms. Another frequent subject of litigation was the mixed marriages ; it had been the policy of the Jesuits to bring these about as often as possible[2], in order that Protestant husbands might be converted by Catholic wives, or at least that their children might be brought up as Catholics ; but now that they felt stronger, they induced the courts to refuse to recognise these as valid[3], unless they had been performed in the presence of a priest and several witnesses. Many Protestants were thus almost compelled to conform to the Catholic religion to save their children from the disabilities of illegitimacy. Others were forced into conformity by finding that Church patronage in the hands of Protestants was subject to legal dispute. Thus by all the means in its power the government favoured the Catholic reaction. ' A Protestant prince,' it was said at Rome, ' a prince who would have distributed high and honourable places among both parties equally, would have filled the whole country with heresy ; for in an age so selfish as this, private interests are too strong for religious attachments ; but since the king had displayed so much constancy, the nobles had learned to obey his will[4].'

A strong party was thus formed through the king and

---

[1] Ranke, ii. 276.   [2] Krasinski.   [3] Ranke, ii. 276.   [4] Ibid.

Senate, of which the Jesuits were the moving spirits ; in
Party of Re- religion it was devoted to the Catholic reaction ;
action.   in politics it supported the king and government
against the encroachments of the lesser gentry [1]. If this
latter object had been pursued with a view to national
interests and by lawful means, no policy would have been
more beneficial to Poland ; for a strong government, even
had it been Roman Catholic, would have done much to
avert the ruin of Poland, of which the turbulence of the
lesser nobility was one of the principal causes ; but the
power of the monarchy was utilised solely in the interests of
Rome and the Jesuits, with the result that while the influence
of the latter steadily increased, the authority of the monarch
as steadily declined, and a party which might have done
good service in the organisation of Poland was employed
merely for the advantage of the Jesuits.

This party, as it was twofold in character, met with a two-
The Opposi- fold opposition, political and religious. It was
tion.   said that whenever the king bestowed an honour,
it made one ungrateful noble and a hundred discontented.
These latter naturally joined with the nuncios, who formed
a standing opposition to the Senate and government. It
was at this time led by Zamoyski, who had made himself the
idol of the lesser nobility by carrying the resolution in 1573,
that not merely the Diet but every Polish gentleman should
share in the election of their kings ; and to this party the
Protestants joined themselves. The proceedings of the

---

[1] Compare Skarga's address to the king at the Diet of Warsaw, 1606.
'Eheu Rex, quorsum jam nobis res tua intempestiva conniventia reci-
derunt ? Reges olim Poloniae de rebus ad Rempublicam spectantibus
cum solis senatoribus deliberabant, nunciorum istorum terrestrium, quos
vocant, nullae in hisce rebus, partes erant ut qui non ita dudum intro-
ducti sunt. Nunc vero tua et quorundam majorum tuorum socordia res
eo, proh dolor, deducta est ut quam primum ferculus aliquis domicellus
qui se pro nuncio terrestri gerit, votum suum proponit, omnes ei protinus
assurgere conantur. Tuum erat hujusmodi perversas consuetudines quae
contra antiquos mores inoleverunt cohibere.' Mercure Jesuite, ' Consilium de recuperanda pace regni Poloniae.'

Rokosz of 1607 illustrate alike its aims and its twofold composition ; they are not agreed on the subject of the Jesuits : the Catholics complain of the encroachments of the Society on their prerogatives [1], but their Catholicism prevents them from supporting the project of the Protestants, that they should be expelled from the country [2] ; and this diversity probably contributed no little to the success of the king. The bishops were also a subject of common hatred to the Protestants because of their spiritual, to the Catholics because of their temporal power ; and another frequent complaint was [3] that through the Jesuits ' strangers and men of obscure birth entered upon the goods of the country.' The defeat of this party did not have the effect that might have been expected ; the Protestants indeed were reduced to impotence, and declined more rapidly after the battle of Guzow, even than they had done before ; persecution was given a free hand, and the influence of the Jesuits was more than ever firmly established. But this victory on the part of the king produced no political or constitutional effects whatever ; the lesser nobility became more decisively Catholic, but their power and independence was as great as ever ; the monarchy possessed no more influence than it had done before, and the disintegrating tendencies in Poland pursued their course unchecked. Sigismund was incapable of utilising the victory he had gained for the benefit of the monarchy, but the Jesuits were quite skilful enough to employ to the full the advantages which it secured to them and to the Roman Catholic Church : it was probably in part due to them that the king did not reap the political fruits of his victory.

They were quite alive to the possibility of a king who was hostile to them succeeding to the throne ; and in the hands

---

[1] Cf. also the speeches on the Cracow question at the Diet of Warsaw, March 4, 1626.   [2] Thuanus, v. 1300.

[3] Argentus, and ' Oratio Equitis Poloni contra Soc. Jesu,' ante chap. vi.

of such a king a strong monarchical power would not be desirable, and they took care that no such power should be created. The accession of Ladislas and his attempts to reduce the influence of the Society fully justified these precautions.

CHAPTER X.

Influence of the Society upon Foreign Relations of Poland.

It has always been one of the disadvantages of Roman Catholic countries, that their foreign policy has been liable to interference from a power which looks not so much to the particular interests of each nation as to the general interests of a would-be universal Church. This was especially the case during the contest between the Roman Catholic Church and the Reformation, when the energies of the former were solely directed to the extirpation of the latter. The chosen instruments in this work were the Jesuits, whose primary *raison d'être* was unquestioning obedience to the Papal will. From the time when they gained firm hold of the government of Poland, that country ceased to be much more than the northern agent of Rome and the house of Austria. It was used as a basis of operations against states like Sweden and Russia, and naturally reaped the fruits of its influence in those countries, when they in their turn became powerful enough to avenge upon Poland the miseries it had inflicted upon them.

Poland was in a unique position : it was the only State in the north of Europe which owned the supremacy of the Roman Pontiff. Its main object should, there- Relations with fore, have been to strengthen its internal re- Russia. sources in the face of its enemies, and refrain from needless intervention in the affairs of its heretic and schismatic neighbours. Its actual course was to lend itself to the designs of Rome upon Sweden and Russia, while its internal affairs went rapidly from bad to worse. Its most important dealings were with the rival Slav power in the East, which Ivan the Third and Ivan the Terrible had freed from the Tatar yoke, and raised on the ruins of Viatka and Novgorod to the position of a European power. In a war which had broken out about Livonia, Batory was carrying all before him, when Ivan determined to invite the Pope to mediate peace, holding out hopes of his conversion to the Church of Rome. Gregory XIII acceded with alacrity to the proposal, and despatched the most accomplished diplomatist the Society of Jesus then possessed to the court of Moscow. Antonio Possevino [1]

Possevino. was born at Mantua in 1534, became secretary to Gonzaga, and after considerable success in various secular missions, resolved to enter the Society of Jesus. He was first employed to bring about an accommodation with the revolted heretics of Valais and Piedmont. For the next few years his activity was confined to various affairs in France, but in 1577 he was sent to effect the conversion of John King of Sweden; on the failure of this attempt he proceeded to Poland, where he became one of the most active and zealous promoters of the Catholic reaction. He founded colleges at Wilna [2] and Dorpat, and a seminary at Braunsberg, which was attached to the college there. At the command of Gregory he set out at once for Moscow, where he was received with great pomp by the Tsar, who, however, was more than a match for the supple Jesuit. In the firm persuasion that Ivan would establish Roman Catholicism in Russia, Possevino undertook to obtain from Batory very favourable terms of peace. The king of Poland

---

[1] 'Vie du Père Possevin.' Paris, 1712.

[2] Ibid., and 'Vicissitudes de l'Eglise Catholique en Pologne,' with preface by Montalembert.

was engaged on the siege of Pskov, and was very anxious to capture the place. 'Nevertheless[1],' in the words of one of the historians of the Society, 'he gave up great advantages out of love for the Church,' and Pskov remained in the hands of Ivan : though Poland secured Polock and Livonia, the peace was an inestimable advantage to Muscovy. Possevino now returned to Moscow, to complete the conversion of the Tsar and procure the establishment of the Jesuits in the country. But his proselytising zeal met with no more success than Rohita[2] and the English merchants had done in their endeavours to win over Ivan to Protestantism. The Tsar had strong religious or irreligious opinions of his own, and declined to exchange them for either Catholic or Protestant dogmas, and now that he had obtained the peace he wanted, there was no longer any reason for concealing the fact. The second of these objects was not more prosperous : 'the demand,' said Ivan, 'was useless, because the Jesuits would never succeed in converting Russia, and besides, it would require twenty Jesuits to deceive one Russian, so all their trouble would be lost[3].' The Tsar does not seem to have formed a very favourable opinion of the Jesuit, and after his departure called him a wolf[4]. Possevino now returned to Poland, where he furthered the interests of the Society by his influence at the court, advocated the union with the Greek Church, and occupied himself with the affairs of the King of Poland, 'by the order of the Holy See' his biographer is careful to explain[5]. The attempt upon the Eastern Church in Russia by means of diplomacy having failed, the Jesuits turned with better success their attention to that in Poland ; but they had by no means abandoned the idea of converting Russia, and the appearance of the false Demetrius gave

---

[1] Crétineau-Joly, vol. ii. p. 346. [2] Morfill, 'History of Russia.'
[3] Léonard Chodzko, quoted by Lelewel, 'Hist. de la Lithuanie.'
[4] Karamsin, ix. v. [5] 'Vie du Père Possevin.'

them a golden opportunity. The whole story of the origin
Demetrius. of this extraordinary adventurer is wrapped in
mystery[1]; but whatever it may have been,
the Jesuits supported him with all the means at their
disposal. It was to a Jesuit that he first revealed his
supposed identity : he undertook to make the union of
the two Churches and promotion of religion his chief care
if he were placed upon the throne of the Tsars. The
matter was at first concealed, but the Pope was advised
to further by his own resources and influence with the
King and magnates of Poland, an enterprise which concerned the interests of religion and aggrandisement of the
Holy See. This was sedulously done by the Jesuits ; they
introduced the suppliant to George Mniszek, Palatine of
Sandomir, who gave him his daughter Marina in marriage.
He was next brought into the presence of Sigismund, to
whom he related the story of his imprisonment and escape.
An army was collected by the aid of the Jesuits. Boris sent
an embassy to Poland to expose the pretender, but could not
prevail over the influence of the Pope and the Jesuits, two of
whom accompanied the Polish army to Moscow. The advantages of his success would indeed have been enormous
both for Poland and for Rome. The former would have a
friend and ally, instead of a dangerous enemy, and the Pope
would have a devoted son, instead of an obstinate schismatic.
This probably explains the ready credulity of Sigismund
and the Jesuits[2]. Demetrius abjured his Greek religion

---

[1] According to Rambaud, Otrepièff was a Greek monk who had early
predicted his elevation to the throne : if this is correct it is impossible
that the Jesuits should have hatched the whole plot. But it is equally
evident that they espoused his cause with zeal from the account of
Thuanus, who seems inclined to believe that Demetrius was genuine.
Part v. 519, 1199, 1203, 1219, 1220, &c. Cf. Morfill, who thinks the
Jesuits took advantage of the opportunity, as also does Karamsin.
Ranke likewise, ii. 272. Margeret. however, who was in Russia at the
time, denies this ; and Father Pierling in his ' Rome et Demetrius' has
recently attempted to absolve the Society and the Pope from complicity
in this scheme. [2] Karamsin.

at a Jesuit house in Cracow, and Clement VIII hastened
to assure him that he was ready to use in his favour all the
spiritual power which heaven had granted to the vicar of
St. Peter[1]. After his coronation at Moscow, the Jesuits
congratulated Demetrius on his success, and were granted
a habitation not far from the citadel[2]. They were, however,
soon expelled, and a proclamation was issued declaring
that Demetrius was really a monk named Otrepièff, and
exposing letters from him to the Pope, and his promises
to the Jesuits[3]. If these latter had given the pretender
great assistance, their undue haste to establish Romanism in
Moscow was one of the principal causes of his speedy down-
fall. 'The conduct of the Jesuits with regard to Demetrius,'
wrote a Roman Catholic Bishop[4] to Possevino, 'had been
most unfortunate. If he were the true Demetrius, it was
not prudent to expose him to ruin by their perfervid
counsels before he was well seated on the throne, and to
involve so many of the flower of Polish nobility in his fall;
if he were false[5], their action had been most nefarious in
thinking that a good cause had need of a glaring and
detestable fraud.' Then followed a period which the
Russians justly call the Time of Troubles. A second
Demetrius imitated the first: he was supported by a large
number of Poles, though they knew he was false[6]. Again
and again the Poles took advantage of the weakness of
Russia and meditated its partition; Ladislas[7] was crowned
king at Moscow, but the eagerness of Sigismund to acquire
Russia for himself caused his son's failure. Their conduct
was long remembered by the Russians. It deepened the
bitterness of the rivalry between the two Slavonic nations

---

[1] Karamsin, vol. x.   [2] Thuanus, part v. 1203.
[3] Thuanus, part v. 1219, 1220.
[4] Stanislas Przowski, quoted by Thuanus, part v, 1264 A. B.
[5] Piasecius is more reticent on this question, but Mouraiveff, 'Hist. of
Russian Church,' naturally agrees with Karamsin.
[6] Piasecius, p. 253.   [7] Continuation of Thuanus, p. 235.

and the hatred of Russia for Rome ; this feeling is illustrated by the Journal of Macarius[1], Patriarch of Antioch, who visited Russia at this time. To the Russians Poland became the chief representative of the Latin Church[2]; Papal supremacy was in the national mind identified with Polish conquest.

Russia was not the only country with which Poland was embroiled by its proselytising zeal on behalf of Rome. An Attempt on attempt had been made by the Jesuits to bring Sweden. back Sweden to the orthodox fold during the reign of John, Sigismund's father. But Possevino's influence could not prevail upon that monarch to re-establish Romanism in face of the determined opposition of the nation ; and the hopes of Rome were deferred, till in 1592 Sigismund, who had been educated by his mother Catherine in Roman Catholic tenets in order to secure the throne of Poland, became by the death of his father king of Sweden. He was bound by his coronation oath not to injure the Church of the country, but these promises soon gave way before his consuming zeal on behalf of Rome. The influence of the Catholics began to increase ; but they were in a very small minority, and the Protestants found a leader in the king's uncle Charles, and during Sigismund's absence in Poland Protestantism was re-established. Sigismund now appealed to arms, but was completely defeated at Stangebro in 1598.

In these disastrous enterprises Poland was acting chiefly as the cat's-paw of the house of Austria. Its dependence Subservience upon that power was a circumstance which to Austria. writers, Catholic as well as Protestant, contemporary and modern, with one voice deplore. 'Poland,' says an author[3] already quoted, 'had joined the league of

---

[1] Some of it is quoted by Stanley, 'Eastern Church,' p. 328.

[2] Ibid.

[3] 'Consilium de recuperanda pace regni Poloniae,' Mercure Jesuite, 1626.

Princes, and especially Austria, to execute the decrees of
the Council of Trent, and this was the cause of all her
woes.' 'The alliance with Austria,' echoes Salvandy[1], 'was
the cause of innumerable evils, and introduced into Poland
the repressive spirit of Vienna.' 'Ill-starred,' wrote Stanislas
Przowski[2], 'were the counsels given by the Jesuits to the
king from the beginning; through them it was that he
visited, at great risk of his life, his hereditary kingdom,
abandoned, and finally lost it. Nor was his second[3]
marriage negotiated by the Jesuits more fortunate, after the
celebration of which, the kingdom, before quiet, was disturbed with unwonted commotions.' 'The Jesuits,' said
the manifesto[4] of the Rokosz in 1606, 'caused alliances
and marriages to be contracted with the House of Austria,
by means of which they had all Poland in their power.'
In 1597 Mendoza was sent to cement the peace between
the two countries, and a Jesuit named Thomas Sallius
accompanied him; they had another object, viz. to persuade
Sigismund to give up the use of the title 'Defender of the
Faith,' which he still employed in addressing the Queen of
England, and to counteract the wiles which that country
was accused of spreading all over Poland[5]. Some time
before the English had proposed a treaty of commerce with
Poland, which promised to be very advantageous, especially
to Dantzic, but the Roman Catholic Nuncio prevented its
conclusion, chiefly because the English required the most
distinct promise that they should be allowed to trade in
peace without molestation on account of their religion[6].
The Jesuits also persuaded Sigismund to make war on the
Turks, contrary to the advice of Zamoyski[7]; and this use
of Poland as the cat's-paw of Rome, in its relations with

---

[1] 'Hist. de Pologne avant et sous Jean Sobieski.
[2] Thuanus, v. 1264.
[3] I.e. with another Austrian princess of the line of Grätz.
[4] Thuanus, v. 1299.   [5] Ibid. 730 E.
[6] Ranke, ii. 256.   [7] Thuanus, v. 731.

Turkey, became a fruitful source of disaster and loss to the kingdom. The same baleful influence induced Sigismund to aid Austria against the Bohemians during the Thirty Years War, a policy as opposed to racial feeling as it was to national interests, because it was a Slav power aiding a German ruler to crush a Slav nationality. It was no strange thing that, guided in a path like this by influences so baleful, Poland sank rapidly in fifty years from a position in which it was a danger to its neighbours, to a state in which it was possible for these same neighbours to overrun it almost without opposition.

CHAPTER XI.

SUPREMACY OF THE SOCIETY IN POLAND.

IT has been the usual practice to write of the Society of Jesus in one of two ways : its apologists are apt to maintain that the zeal, purity, and devotion which cha- Change in racterised it in its earliest days, remained un- the Society. corrupted and unalloyed all through its history, till it was suppressed by Clement XIV. On the other hand, those to whom Jesuitism is a 'consecrated falsity' and 'light of hell[1],' persist in crediting the founders of the Society with all the vileness and worldliness into which its members sank in the eighteenth century. Neither is a very scientific method of historical criticism ; if it is an accepted maxim that nothing which is wholly a lie ever leads and attracts the best minds of any generation, it is also true that 'the old order changes,' that as the beauty and strength of physical life do not escape dissolution, so the purest and best of religious forms and ideals tend towards corruption and decay. This is what happened in the Society of Jesus. Whatever be the judgment pronounced upon the effects which Jesuit methods and ideas produced in Poland and elsewhere, it is idle to deny the disinterested motives of the founders and pioneers of the Society. But by the middle of the seventeenth century innovations had crept in which impaired the original purity of the Order[2]. More than half a century before, Mariana had exposed these tendencies to

---

[1] Carlyle, ' Latter Day Pamphlets.'   [2] Ranke, vol. iii. pp. 89, 90.

evil, he complained that houses of probation had been founded not under the control of colleges, where life was too easy, and the novices ran into debt and neglected their services; their professions of charity and humility were empty words. The coadjutors were usurping the privileges of the professed; the Society was undertaking to manage farms and other temporal concerns; other sources of evil were the system of secret information and the excessive power of the General[1]. The greatest change was, however, that the original distinction between the 'professed' and the coadjutors was obliterated; the former, who were really bound to live on alms and devote themselves exclusively to spiritual work, began to acquire fixed revenues and temporal power. Hence the missionary enterprise and apostolic poverty of the Jesuits gave way to a desire for temporal authority; their activity became more conspicuous in political intrigues and commercial speculations than in the salvation of souls or conversion of heretics, for which ends they began to rely more on the secular power than on their own efforts. This degeneration was no less conspicuous in Poland than elsewhere. As early as 1600 the increasing number of the coadjutors is apparent from the statistics in the Annual Letters of the Society, and the ease with which the Society gained possession of the secular power led quickly to its application in the work of converting heretics and schismatics. Its eagerness to acquire wealth is illustrated by the proceedings at the Diet of Grodno in 1679, concerning the possessions of the Society at Iaroslav, where its members were accused of continual usurpations of the property of their neighbours. 'It is with great grief,' wrote Sobieski, who was a great patron of the Society, to its General, 'that I see you, by your eagerness to extend your

---

[1] Mariana on the Defects of the Government of the Society, 'Mercure Jesuite,' 1626. 1630. He was leading the attack on Acquaviva, and would probably exaggerate these defects.

property beyond all limits and all rights, do violence to the regard for the Society, with which its great services towards the Church of God have inspired me. I do not wish to have your brothers of Iaroslav judged before the Diet. I should fear to envenom still more the hatred, already too great, which the estates of the realm bear towards you. My interest and affection make it my duty to engage your devotion to attempt to remedy growing evils, and to keep off from the Jesuits of Poland the contagion of ambitious and avaricious passions which are only too manifest elsewhere. Distrust this too frequent change of rectors in your colleges ; from fear of losing caste with the Order, and of not leaving monuments of their tenure of office, they struggle to enrich their establishment by all possible means ; this is their only care and anxiety [1].'

The accession of Ladislas brought a little relief to the Protestants after the long reign of Sigismund : the new king was averse to persecution, and refused to tolerate the Jesuits at his court. He did what he could to ameliorate the condition of the adherents of the Eastern Church, and his personal influence deferred for a few years the revolt of the Cossacks. But the royal power had by this time lost all substance, and the kings were in much the same position of the typical 'roi fainéant' of the later Merovings. Ladislas wished to marry the daughter of Frederick, Elector Palatine, but the opposition of the Jesuits to a Protestant alliance was too strong, and he had to relinquish the idea. He was equally unable to save the Dissidents, as the Protestants were now erroneously called, from persecution, and was often forced to promulgate decrees exclusively in the interests of the Roman Catholics. At the election Diet of 1632, it was decreed that the Protestants should have free use of the churches they already possessed, but should not build in new places, though they might

Ladislas.

---

[1] Salvandy.

enjoy private worship where they liked[1]. In 1640 a decree
of the Diet at Warsaw deprived the Protestants of Wilna of
all their establishments in that city, and prohibited all
exercise of their worship[2]. Radziwill complained that it
was no longer merely the dregs of the people or unruly
students, but the secular arm and nobles of the highest rank,
who were employed against the Protestants[3]. At Lublin a
mob attacked a Protestant funeral, and the Protestants killed
two in self-defence ; the king gave Mukowski, the chief
Protestant in the city, a royal letter by which he was
sheltered from any judicial prosecution[4]; nevertheless
the supreme tribunal cited him to appear, and condemned
him to death in defiance of the royal authority. In 1637
at Cracow[5] the bishop directed each householder to declare
how many heretics he had in his dwelling, and this was
made the pretext of frequent invasions of their houses by
Jesuits on Ascension Day, while their activity in attacking
Protestant churches was undiminished. Nevertheless, the
king and his chancellor, Ossolinski, made an attempt to
bring about an understanding between the various churches
of Poland. For this purpose a 'colloquium charitativum'
was convened at Thorn in August, 1645; from this the
Socinians were excluded. From the first disagreements
arose, and the colloquium soon broke up without any result[6].
In 1648, at an evil moment for Poland, Ladislas died, and
Casimir.   was succeeded by his brother John Casimir.
During his reign[7] Poland was overrun by
Swedes, Turks and Russians, and only disagreement among
its enemies prevented the anticipation of its dismemberment

[1] Wengerscius, p. 247.   [2] Ibid. p. 257.   [3] Ibid. p. 259.
[4] Krasinski, 'Reformation in Poland,' ii. 234.
[5] Wengerscius, p. 235.   [6] Ibid. p. 99.
[7] Crétineau-Joly, that veracious and impartial historian of the Society,
gives the following account of his reign : 'He silenced the factions
which divided the kingdom, and when he judged that his mission was
completed, he abdicated in 1668. His reign was one of peace and
public education !' Crétineau-Joly, vol. iv. p. 132.

by more than a century. Casimir was a Jesuit, and had been made a cardinal by Innocent X, but this dignity he resigned, and the Pope absolved him from his vows [1]. His election met with considerable opposition from the bishop of Kiev and others, including of course the Protestants, who objected on the score of his being a monk. The Jesuits regarded him less as a king than as a faithful brother of their Order [2], and under his sway regained that supremacy which had been somewhat impaired by the rule of Ladislas: their influence was, however, only signalised by increased persecution and renewed disasters. Casimir gave himself over to the influence of Jesuits and mistresses [3]. His persecution brought about the revolt of the Cossacks, and his intrigue with the wife of his chancellor was the occasion of the war with Sweden. The expulsion of the Swedes was followed by a fresh onslaught on the Protestants, who were accused of abetting their cause. The Socinians, who had already been deprived of their celebrated school at Rakow, were in 1658 expelled by the Diet at the instigation of a Jesuit name Karwat [4], merely for theological reasons, and in spite of their attempt at the colloquium at Roznow to show that there was little difference in doctrine between them and the Roman Catholic Church. The condition of the country is forcibly illustrated by a pamphlet published anonymously in 1665 [5], which, speaking in the name of Poland, professes its zeal for the establishment of one religion not only in Poland, but all over the world. Poland, it continues, detests heresies and schisms of all kinds, but after once having admitted divers religions and confirmed them by the laws, oaths, and long-established custom of the realm, it would have wished that liberty once granted on public faith should have been preserved inviolate for one

---

[1] Connor.   [2] Salvandy.   [3] Ibid.   [4] Krasinski.
[5] 'Moriens Polonia suos et exteros alloquitur,' 1665, October. This is a curious little brochure of about eight pages; a copy is in the Bodleian. It is anonymous, and the place of publication is not given.

and all.   Of all the evils that encompassed the country, the
revolt of the Cossacks was the worst, and who could doubt
that the Cossacks were irritated against Poland by the
wrongs done to the Greek religion?   It could not look for
help from God, whose name it had taken in vain as often as
it had been invoked in guaranteeing peace and liberty to all.
It was imperative to restore to the Cossacks and the Dissidents the rights and privileges they had enjoyed before, to
keep peace and faith with them, and by their help make war
on external enemies.

During the short and inglorious reign of Michael, Poland
was a prey to civil war; the Jesuits supported the Paz faction
in order to maintain their influence over the country[1].   The
ruin of Poland was postponed for a century by the victories

Sobieski.
of Sobieski, but his policy was not very enlightened at home or abroad.   Though averse
to persecution, he was unable to repress the excessive zeal
of the Jesuits, or enforce the laws which still verbally maintained religious liberty.   On April 2, 1682, a mob led on by
the Jesuits attacked and pillaged a church which the Protestants had built in the neighbourhood, after their expulsion
from Wilna [2].   The case of Casimir Lyszczinski [3] painfully
illustrates the religious temper of Catholicism in Poland, at
a time when the Jesuits were at the height of their power.
Lyszczinski had written on the margin of a work, in which
the author's arguments in favour of the existence of God
were unintelligible, the ironical comment 'ergo non est
Deus.'   This circumstance was discovered and denounced
by one of his debtors; two bishops, Witwicki and Zaluski,
took up the matter with great zeal, and the Diet of 1689
condemned Lyszczinski to have his tongue torn out, be
beheaded, and then burnt.   This barbarous sentence was

[1] Salvandy.   [2] Krasinski.
[3] Krasinski has taken his account almost word for word from
Salvandy.

executed in spite of the efforts of the king, who declared that the Spanish Inquisition had done nothing worse, and the Pope himself expressed his abhorrence of the deed.

The only parts where Protestants survived were Polish Prussia, Courland and some of the towns, such as Posen, &c. The Jesuits had been expelled from Dantzic[1], but succeeded in re-establishing a mission there during the early part of the eighteenth century. In Mittau[2], they pretended to have bought a living, but the Calvinist population was strong enough to pillage their college and render their existence precarious. Elsewhere the progress of the Society had been marvellously rapid. At the beginning of the century it had establishments at seventeen different places[3]; before the end this number had been multiplied fourfold. In 1600 there were four hundred and sixty-six Jesuits in Poland; at the end of Sobieski's reign there were more than seventeen hundred. It is this proportion of Jesuits to the population, far greater than that in any other country of Europe, which makes it justifiable to attribute to their influence the political, social, and religious condition of Poland at this time. Their influence still inclined Poland towards the Austrian alliance[4]; one of the signs of degeneration in the Society was the prominence of its members at the courts of kings. The example of Lachaise in France and Peters in England was imitated by Vota, who succeeded Przebowski as confessor to John Sobieski. He was sent to open negotiations with Russia about the union of the Greek and Latin Churches, which were no more successful than those of Possevino had been. He then became a sort of prime[5] minister to Sobieski, and determined him to reject the alliance of France and join the League of Augsburg. Poland was the prey of the rival factions of

[1] Salvandy.   [2] Connor, 'Letters on Poland.'
[3] 'Annuae Litterae,' 1600.
[4] Salvandy ; also Guettée and Crétineau-Joly.
[5] Crétineau-Joly, iv. 133.

France and Austria; both powers maintained parties in the Diet, and the latter, by the influence of the bishops and Jesuits, induced Poland to declare war upon the Turks, under the guise of religion. While it lost the sympathy of France, which might have saved it from partition in the next century, Poland reaped no advantage from the alliance with Austria; the victories of Sobieski and deliverance of Vienna brought it nothing but barren glory, and the country for which it made these sacrifices was none the less glad to share in its plunder in 1772 and 1795.

The social influence of the Jesuits must be judged not so much by what was done as by what was not done. In the fifteenth century the Poles had been perhaps the most educated and cultured nation in Europe; it was indeed a culture which only reached the comparatively small class of gentlemen who lived on the labour of their serfs, but even these by the seventeenth century were sinking as fast into ignorance as the other countries of Europe were rising out of it. The predominance of the Jesuits seemed to have taken all originality and all growth out of the Poles; there was no such thing as progress; all was stagnation or re-action. There was less and less opposition to the Society in Poland, and its history becomes less and less eventful; it had become supreme in Poland as it never became supreme in any other country in Europe.

CHAPTER XII.

Decline and Fall.

THE eighteenth century was a period of decline and fall alike for Poland and the Society of Jesus. The victories of Sobieski made observers[1] think that in spite of its anarchy Poland would yet last a long while; but its vigour was more apparent than real; the Poles could still fight, but they could do nothing else. The force of the government had become so attenuated that Poland presented the appearance of a heterogeneous conglomeration of autonomous States somewhat resembling the Empire without the larger powers, like Prussia, Bavaria, Saxony, &c.; the system of 'mandats impératifs,' combined with the 'liberum veto,' reduced the Diet to absolute impotence. The Saxon dynasty did nothing towards reform, and was content to reign by the grace of Russia. The transient success of Stanislas Leszczinski and his patron, Charles XII, roused the hopes of the Protestants, but Pultava restored the Saxon dynasty and domination of Russia. This country now began to make the acquisition of Poland its chief aim, and used the Saxon kings as its instruments. The Treaty of Warsaw, negotiated by Szaniawsky[2] in 1716, illustrated the double character of its policy; Poland was disarmed by the reduction of its army, and at the same time the prohibition of the worship of the Dissidents in all churches except those built before the decrees of 1632, secured the

---

[1] E. g. Connor, 'Letters on Poland.'   [2] Krasinski.

maintenance of a discontented party, ever ready to look abroad for help. So great was the ascendancy of Russia, that Poles who wished for preferment flocked to the court of St. Petersburg to obtain it through Russian mediation. The Jesuits in the meantime, in spite of the growing corruption of the Society, were still increasing their influ-

Extent of the ence and numbers in Poland. At the time of
Society in the suppression of the Society there were in
Poland. the two provinces of Poland and Lithuania two thousand and ninety-seven members of the Society, and the Society possessed establishments at more than a hundred and fifty different places[1]. Their régime was marked by no increase of toleration. The Treaty of Warsaw placed the Dissidents in a worse legal position than they had been before ; in 1718 a Protestant nuncio, Piotrowski, was prevented from taking his seat in the Diet, though there was no law to exclude him, and two instances of persecution occurred about this time, which showed that Poland had become the most intolerant country in Europe. In 1715

Case of Sigismund Unruh was condemned to have his
Unruh. tongue torn out, his right hand cut off, and burnt, for writing a sentence which was interpreted as blasphemy. His flight prevented the execution of this sentence, which the Pope proclaimed null and void on the

Massacre ground of technical informality. The second
of Thorn. case caused a great sensation in Europe, and had no small effect in producing the indifference, or rather acclamation, with which liberal Europe received the partition of Poland half a century later. This was the famous massacre of Thorn. In July, 1724, a fight took place between some Jesuits and a number of Protestant boys. The authorities seized one of the Jesuits, who in their turn

[1] Guettée, vol. iii, table at the end. These numbers are for the Jesuit provinces of Poland and Lithuania, which included Transylvania and such places as Constantinople, &c. The number in Poland would be about 1900, and their establishments between 120 and 130.

captured a Protestant boy, whom they refused to deliver up. This caused great excitement, and a crowd liberated the boy, without, however, committing any excesses; but they were shot at, and then seized the furniture of the college and burnt it. The Jesuits now began to agitate, and demanded that the city, with its Protestant establishments, should be handed over to the Romanists. They took every means to rouse the bigotry of the country, with such success that the constituencies commanded their representatives to avenge the offended majesty of God. A commission of ecclesiastics and laymen was appointed by the king to investigate the matter; this enquiry was managed by the Jesuits, and only witnesses presented by them were heard. More than sixty persons were imprisoned, and the affair was brought before the Assessional Court, which was the supreme tribunal of appeal for the towns. It consisted of the first judicial officers of the State, but they were swamped by the addition of forty new members, chosen under the influence of the Jesuits. The decree pronounced condemned Roesner, president of the town council, to be beheaded, and his property confiscated, although his alleged crime was only a failure to do his duty in repressing the riot; the vice-president and twelve burghers, accused of having incited the riot, were condemned to the same penalty, whilst several individuals were condemned to fines, imprisonment, and corporal punishment. It was also ordered that half the city council and militia, with all its officers, should consist of Roman Catholics; the college of the Protestants was to be given them, as well as the church of St. Mary. The Protestants could only have schools outside the walls, and print with the approbation of the Roman Catholic bishop. The Diet confirmed this decree; but before it could be executed it was necessary for the Jesuits to confirm by oath the facts presented in the indictment, which it was imagined their sacred calling would prevent them from doing. They, however, managed to overcome their scruples, and Roesner, with eleven others, was executed. This sentence called forth protestations from several European powers, but these only brought odium upon the Protestants, who were regarded as the enemies of their country, and in 1732 a law was passed prohibiting them from holding any public office. These

Decline of Poland.

years were among the darkest in Polish history, for after the accession of Poniatowski, in 1764, a national revival was attempted, under the leadership of the Czartoryskis ; how far it was a genuine renascence has been and still is a matter of dispute [1] ; but at least it was an advance upon the state of darkness and ignorance which had prevailed since the time of Sigismund III. It was heralded by an educational reform begun by the Pierists or Patres Pii, of whom Konarski was the chief leader, which aimed at counteracting the effects of the Jesuit system upon education and literature ; its importance was however soon dwarfed by the struggle which had to be waged for national existence. Catherine made a dexterous use of the Dissidents [2] as a pretext for interference in Polish affairs ; she was careful, however, to prevent any measures conducive to national unity in Poland. Her aim was to get virtual possession of the whole of Poland under guise of a protectorate, but the diplomacy of Frederick the Great compelled her to share the booty and consent to a scheme of partition. The share of the Jesuits in these proceedings was small ; it has indeed been asserted that they overcame the scruples of Maria Theresa about accepting a share of the country [3], but this has been met by a declaration that they sent embassies to Vienna on purpose to prevent its execution [4]. In fact they had quite enough to do in their

---

[1] Karéiev, ‘Revue Historique,’ 1891.
[2] Ruhlière, ‘Histoire de l’Anarchie de Pologne,’ vols. i, ii.
[3] Lelewel.　　　　[4] ‘Vicissitudes de l’Église Catholique en Pologne.’

attempts to avoid their own impending ruin. The bankruptcy of La Valette and consequent revelations had shaken the Society to its foundations. It was the object of unceasing attacks from the liberal move- Fall of the ment which, inaugurated in France by Voltaire and the Jesuits. Encyclopaedists, was spreading to every country in Europe, and it was an object of suspicion to the enlightened rulers of that age of paternal despots. The transference of Paraguay from Spain to Portugal was the occasion of their fall; the Fathers who had there established a model theocratic government resisted, and Pombal replied by expelling the Order from Portugal. Charles III and d'Aranda followed suit in Spain, Tanucci in Naples, Choiseul in France, and in 1773 Clement XIV, by his famous bull 'Dominus ac Redemptor,' suppressed the Society. The Jesuits, far from submitting, took refuge with Frederick and Catherine; they elected several Poles in succession as generals, and still directed Polish education [1], while forged Briefs [2] appeared sanctioning their existence; but these questions and the subsequent history of the Society lie beyond the limits [3] of this Essay.

[1] 'Vicissitudes de l'Église Catholique en Pologne.'
[2] These Briefs were contradicted by other genuine ones: for the Jesuit view of the question, see 'The Month,' Nov. 1874.
[3] Viz. 1786, the death of Frederick the Great.

CONCLUSION.

THE dramatic περιπέτεια in the history of Poland has been so striking, and the estimates of the influence of the Jesuits upon it so various, that a sketch of the history of the Society in Poland, on however modest a plan, could have no pretensions to completeness without some attempt to gauge their accuracy. Roughly speaking, there may be said to have been three main causes for the fall of Poland, its incurable anarchy, the indifference felt by the peasantry for the fate of a country which secured to the vast majority of its inhabitants no privileges but a great amount of hardship, and a similar indifference on the part of the Dissidents. The chronological accident by which the House of Jagiellon came to an end about the same time as the Jesuits were introduced into Poland, has given the enemies of the latter an excellent opportunity for attributing to the Society of Jesus the evils which were really due to the extinction of the reigning line, and consequent advance towards anarchy in the already disorganised constitution. This process is signalised by the decrees of the Diet of 1573 : the Jesuits were introduced as early as 1564, but the most hostile critic of the Order will fail to see any connection between the two events. It is not denied that the measures adopted by Sigismund III at the instigation of the Jesuits, to secure the success of the Catholic reaction, provoked the Protestants to oppose to the Senate and government the individual rights of each Polish noble, and to seek to extend those privileges at the expense of the executive and central power, and thus indirectly paved the way for an increase of anarchy. That was an accidental result of their position ; and it is not at all certain that, had any one of the Protestant sects gained possession of the royal power, its conduct would not have been very much the same, and have ended in very similar results ; in that, case it might have been the Jesuits who would have sought to extend the individual privileges of the nobles, and used them as a basis of attack upon the king and senate ; and in Poland as in France might have been heard justifications of tyrannicide instead of the praises of obedience. As it was, it may fairly be questioned whether the blame lies at the door of those who used the central power for their own purposes, and not at that of those who likewise for their own ends utilised the elements of anarchy to oppose it. In reality the Jesuits were but slightly and indirectly to blame for the first of the causes of Poland's ruin ; whether from the circumstance that it had never been subject to foreign regimentation, which seems to have played so large a part in the moulding of other European states, or not, its history has been marked by a constant tendency towards anarchy, which its development did not provide it with elements stable enough to resist. At any rate the causes existed long before the introduction of the Jesuits, and would have continued to operate in much the same way had the Society never been founded. It is much the same with the second cause, namely, the miserable position of the peasantry. To say this, however, is not to absolve the Jesuits from all complicity in these causes of Poland's ruin. It must be granted that the Society sought 'the greater glory of God' without much regard for the national interests of Poland ; but naturally the extension of the kingdom of God would have seemed to them a consummation more devoutly to be wished for than the preservation of the independence of Poland. There is no reason, however, to imagine that they ever felt called upon to make a choice

between the two alternatives, or that the suspicion ever
entered their minds that the policy of the Roman Catholic
reaction was not the best for Poland's temporal as for its
spiritual welfare. Their complicity was due rather to sins
of omission than sins of commission ; that, with the influence it possessed in Poland, literature languished, education was paralysed, reform burked, and Poland remained as
ever 'for the noble a paradise, for the peasant a hell,' is no
light testimony, not to what the Society did to ruin Poland,
but to what it failed to do to save it. Still more serious
was its share in producing the indifference of the Dissidents
to the fate of their country ; this was directly due to the dark
and intolerant form of Catholicism which animated the
reaction in Poland, and of that reaction the Jesuits were
the pioneers and master-types.

Persecution is not perhaps a very wise policy under any
circumstances ; nevertheless, most countries have at one
time or another pursued it without perilling their national
existence. But when a State consists of a number of
autonomous atoms loosely bound together and ever ready
to fly apart, for one sect to persecute and proscribe another
is to offer direct encouragement to foreign intervention
and to put a premium upon disruption. A final stage of
political fatuity is reached when 'a two-handed engine at
the door, stands ready to smite once and smite no more,'
in the shape of a foreign power sympathising with the
persecuted, claiming them as its rightful subjects and their
land as its rightful inheritance. It was this circumstance
that rendered the intervention of the Jesuits in Poland
peculiarly pernicious, and it is this that makes the history of
the Society in Poland not merely a phase in the religious
history of that country, but an important episode in the
development of Europe.